Swan's Song

D1473028

Pamela Hixon Rhea

Swan's Song

Pamela Hixon Rhea

PUBLISHED BY:
BRENTWOOD CHRISTIAN PRESS
4000 BEALLWOOD AVENUE
COLUMBUS, GEORGIA 31904

Forword

Pam began writing poetry at the age of twenty. We were sitting outside on a Sunday afternoon, in our lounge chairs at the little church that Dad pastored, when we both decided to write a poem. Back then we stayed the day, so we had nothing to do until church that night. That was the very beginning of Pam becoming a poet, for as I recollect it, she just decided she was going to be one. She writes almost everyday, and loves "catching moments in time" as she says of her poems, and "putting life's spirit into very permanent things."

For six years, Pam wrote Children's stories, completing the undergraduate and graduate courses with the *Institute of Children's Literature*, and was accepted for publication in magazines such as *Hopscotch, the Young Crusader* and *Highlights for Children*. She also writes songs, and *New World Publishing*, has recorded some of these. For the past twenty years, Pam's poems have appeared in the local Conway *Log Cabin Democrat*.

Swan's Song's title sprang from the idea in which a swan is said to sing its sweetest song in its darkest hour, an allegory to us singing our brightest song of faith and hope in our hour of death, knowing that for the saved there is a bright eternity ahead!

Pam has also worked in gathering, typing, and organizing poems for our late Mother's, Maxine Spryes Hixon's six recently published books, *Sand and Pearls, Voice of the Heart, Mither, Poetic Potpourri,* and *Hidden Treasure I and II,* which have been placed in America's top fifty universities and colleges. Pam and her Mother enjoyed writing time together; hence, Pam's phrase "her partner in crime."

Other work that Pam has done includes writing courses for history tests for the Baptist State University in Dallas, Texas.

We hope you enjoy and receive a blessing from the poems in this collection.

Swan's Song is a gathering of poems that span the years.

Affectionately,

Tena M. Hixon (Pam's sister)

Dedication:

This book is dedicated to my late beloved Mother, Maxine Spyres Hixon and Dad, Carl W. Hixon, the greatest positive influences of my life. Also, to my dearly departed son, Paul Maxwell Rhea who was the "love of my life," about whom I can say as the poet, "'Tis better to have loved and lost than never to have loved at all.'" In life, they "cheered me on," and I count myself the most fortunate of people to have been blessed by their lives.

Table of Contents

7

Memory Lane

I took a walk down memory lane,
From that first step to start again,
And found that when that walk was through,
I'd love to walk again with you.

Swan's Song

'Tis said a swan sings the sweetest song
In the twilight of her day,
And her voice rings of purest sound,
When nearing the end of the way.

Singing a love for life and its fullness,
Yet, accepting with dignity and grace,
The reality and destiny of death
That each alone must face.

The song in all its splendor
Is so filled with vibrant sound,
That echoes from the waters
And from the hills resound.

And I, who have a heaven
And know God's wondrous power,
Dare I sing less sweetly than
The swan who has no other hour?

With grace may I accept
When life's twilight reaches me,
And remember the swan sings sweetly
Without an eternity.

So I will wear the crown of years
As a tribute to God's power,
And sing my sweetest, brightest song,
In my darkest, dying hour.

He Stepped Down

From mansions to a manger,
From splendor to a Cross,
He left His throne in Glory
To save the world from loss.

Forsaking the light of Heaven
To face "dark Calvary,"
Alone, endured that old rugged Cross,
Sin's shackled souls to free.

He left the riches of Glory,
To wear a mock robe and crown,
Yes, He came to lift us up,
Which meant He must step down.

Are You a Summer Soldier?

What made the mighty oak grow strong?
Was it the wind, the rain, the cold?
Are these the things that shook the tree,
And made its roots take hold?

Do we prosper when the sun is shining,
And no clouds obstruct the day,
Then our strength is much
Because no shadows cast o'er our way?

But, dare we brave on
        when the winter storms of life beset,
Or do we faint beside the way?
Fearful of the coming storm,
That threatens to obstruct our pathway.

If we are ones who stand not firm,
When hope wears thin,
We'll not attain the victory,
In the race of life to win.

We'll not be a sturdy oak,
But, a twig tossed aside,
Oh, how sad to have blossomed in the sunshine,
But, in the snow to have withered and died.

Reflections

Oh, Lord, I see the beauty of Thy creation all about,
In the eagle's masterful flight,
In the delicate grace of the swan,
In the rising sun and twilight shadows,
In the mountain's lofty height,
In the recluse of the secluded brook,
In the newness of spring,
In the shimmering shades of fall,
In the rainbow's bright array,
In the starry moonlit sky.
These, and countless other things, bespeak Thy Handiwork,
For at Thy Word, the heavens and earth were born.
But, most of all I see Thee, Lord, within my very soul,
When You touched my heart and left ...
          the beauty of Thy Son.

Always There

I've met You on life's pathways,
Those of pleasure, those of pain,
As You rode upon the storms,
Your presence was made plain.
Even in the darkest midnight,
When the nightingale sang its song,
I saw the dark clouds break,
And felt my heart made strong.
And when I've walked through valleys,
Though sometimes it seemed I walked alone,
You assured me in a still, small voice
That You watched above Your own.
I've seen You in a stranger's face,
And in the sweetness of a child,
For in giving that "cup of water,"
I've known that You have smiled.
Your design, I've seen in the lilies,
And in the fair beauty of a rose,
And felt Your loving kindness
In the gentle breeze that blows.
You came even unto the garden
As I was knelt in prayer,
And let me know, everywhere I go,
That You are always there.

The Eye of the Storm

Over rugged and perilous terrain,
On a dark and stormy sea,
I always pass safely o'er,
With God's Guiding Hand on me.
A sweet retreat I find
In my Refuge – in my Rock,
Though tempests beat without,
And threatening waves do rock.
By still waters I am led,
I neither doubt nor fear,
Though dangers lurk about,
I know my Savior's near.
I find a table set before
Midst the presence of my foe,
Yet, I'm kept safe within His care –
He knows where my footsteps go.
Often I stand rooted,
As wheat amongst the tares,
And I am kept from many dangers
Unseen and to which I'm unaware.
Thus, I have passed unharmed
And walked on a troubled sea,
My trust is ever staid in Him,
For His Love empowers me.
Though angry waves compass,
Though billows toss and roll,
My cup He always overfills,
For He ever keeps my soul.
My life is cupped within His Hands,
My heart is made ever warm,
For the Master, He keeps me …
In the "eye of the storm."

Man is Fearful Alone

Man is a fearful being
When trying all alone,
Not knowing how to keep his head up high,
But, is swallowed up by sinking sands.

Man is a fearful being,
When trying to stand against the waves,
For they swell and surge,
And soon he drowns.

Man is fearful because he is frail,
Yet, never realizes how frail,
Until a small gust of wind
Wrecks his lifelong plans.

Then fearful man renounces pride,
And reaches for that mighty Hand
That calms the sea, and
Quiets man's longing soul.

It's Thanksgiving Time Again!

It's time to baste the Butterball,
For it's Thanksgiving time again,
So bring out the pumpkin pies,
And let the feast begin!

Thinking of that very first Thanksgiving,
At Plymouth long ago –
The pilgrims and the Indians,
What a bounty God bestowed!

It's a time to be thankful,
For family and friends,
But, most of all for Jesus,
Who our many blessings sends.

A time to reach out to the needy,
And to invite the stranger in …
A time to enjoy togetherness,
As loving hearts do blend.

And how we wish times like these,
Would never, ever end,
It's time to baste the Butterball,
For it's Thanksgiving time again!

Harvest of the Heart

From seeds of friendship sown,
From fond memories known,
From endearments grown,
May be gathered
A rich harvest of the heart.

Thankfulness

All that is dear, hold not lightly,
Reverently stand on hallowed ground.
In awed silence give thanks unto God
For all those cherished things.
Let not one day pass in ingratitude,
Nor one blessing remain uncounted,
But, for every breath of freedom's air we breathe,
Let our anthem His praises sing!

Black Friday ... Blue Monday

Black Friday is an American tradition,
The busiest shopping day of the year,
You feel so "in the pink" that day,
Filled with lots of holiday cheer.

Thinking everyone will be "green" with envy,
At the bargains that you find,
You're up, off and running early,
Even though there is a mile long line.

You're no coward as your face the mob,
No one can call you "yellow,"
Standing the risk of being stampeded,
You're a right "jolly good fellow."

But, you wake up on "blue" Monday
Feeling liked you're half-dead,
When you find you've overspent –
And now you're "in the red!"

The "Magic" of Christmas

Christmas wonders – sights and sounds,
A love that makes the world go 'round.

Peace on earth – goodwill to men,
The Season of giving, here, once again.

Trees, lights and mistletoe,
Sleigh bells ringing in the snow!

Reindeer on rooftops, Santa in sleigh,
Wishing all a Merry Christmas Day!

Fragrant smells of Christmas treats,
Firelight, stockings hung, and tinseled trees,

The Christmas Story told once again,
Of baby Jesus, and the manger scene.

Salvation's wonderful news to share,
Glad tidings of Peace and Goodwill to bear.

Friends and family gathered far and near,
Christmas gifts, and the Christmas tear.

It is for all this Christmas "magic," hearts must pause …
Now, who doesn't believe in Santa Claus?

Santa Never Has to Go

This poem was written about my son, Paul, when he was small. He'd pretty well figured out about Santa Claus not being real, and wanted me to tell him the "truth." When I got through explaining, he replied, "Mama, tell me a whopper!"

Once Santa caught me peeking
Around the Christmas tree,
He turned and asked the question,
"Do you still believe in me?"

"Why, of course, I do, Santa,
Look at all the gifts you bring,
I believe in Rudolph and the elves,
And in all the Christmas things."

He smiled and jolly-ho-hoed,
And shook in a rumble,
Off came his beard, off came his hat,
And I saw my Daddy stumble.

Continued

"Why, you're not Santa Claus," I cried,
"Why did you trick me so?"
Sheepishly, my Dad replied,
"Why, Son, I thought you'd know,

That Santa Claus lives in the hearts
Of both the young and old,
Always give the gifts of love,
And Santa never has to go."

He sadly brushed my falling tear,
And then I heard him say,
"If you listen with your heart,
You might even hear his sleigh."

Now I know his message,
As I fumble down the stairs,
Dressed in Santa "look alikes."
To my daughter unaware.

Someday, she'll know the difference,
But, then, she'll also know,
If you listen with your heart,
Santa never has to go.

Christmas is Nigh!

Sing it loud and clear,
Tell it far and near,
For everyone to hear,
Christmas is nigh!

Feel it in the air,
Its sights and sounds, everywhere,
Gifts of love to share,
Christmas is nigh!

Tinseled trees and mistletoe,
Santa's jolly "Ho-Ho-Ho,"
Busy shoppers "to and fro,"
Christmas is nigh!

Carolers singing in the snow,
Firelight reflecting faces, aglow,
And in all this I know,
Christmas is nigh!

Bearing Salvation's wonderful news,
Ringing out God's Love so true,
The Christmas Story ever new,
Christmas is nigh!

Christmas is nigh!
Christmas is nigh!
See Bethlehem's star light up the sky!
For Christmas is nigh!

Our Christmas

They're trying to rule against Christmas,
It's so sad but it's true,
But, you can't take Christ out of Christmas,
For that will never really do.

For Christ is at the heart of Christmas,
He's the very reason we celebrate,
Unto us a Savior was born,
To save us from Hell's awful fate.

And Christmas will always be,
About giving and sharing our love,
The true meaning of Christmas is,
The precious gift from the Father Above.

At the name of the word "Christmas,"
Hearts gladden and joy-bells ring,
Loud Hosannas in the highest,
His praises we proclaim.

But, you won't back us into a corner long,
For our rebuttal will only say,
These best wishes are being sent,
To have a Happy Holy-Day!

Don't Leave the Christ Out of Christmas

Don't leave the Christ out of Christmas,
For He is the hope, joy, peace and light,
Come, kneel beside the manger
On that Holy Night.

Don't leave the Christ out of Christmas
For He is the Savior unto the world,
In that little town of Bethlehem,
God's banner of love was unfurled.

Don't leave the Christ out of Christmas,
For He makes the season bright,
The Angels announced His advent
And the world was set aright.

Don't leave the Christ out of Christmas,
For it will be a world dark and forlorn,
But, the Messiah hath come,
And unto us the Savior was born.

Though there was no room for Him at the inn,
Give Him room in your heart today,
Put the Christ into Christmas,
And true Christmas joy will come to stay.

The Day "After" Christmas

'Twas the day after Christmas,
With no stirring about,
Empty packages lay strewn –
The garbage needed taking out!

Everyone was grumpy,
Merriment was gone,
Even the family dog,
Growled over his bone.

The chimney was all covered
"With soot,"
There was work to be done,
But, no one wanted to do it!

The kitchen was all cluttered,
With everything in a mess,
It seems Christmas dinner
Was everyone's best.

No one was cheerful,
For credit cards were all "maxed,"
Dad and Mom were so worried,
They could "not relax."

The snowman was melting,
The decorations were falling down,
No music filled the air,
No carolers gathered 'round.

Someone badly needed
To shovel the sidewalk snow,
And the kids were keyed up
With no place to go!

And the Christmas snow,
Had dirty tracks,
And things usually "in sync"
Were all out of whack!

The homeless once again,
Took to the streets,
As if "one day" of charity
Was all they would need.

No prancing on rooftops
By reindeer and sleigh,
Christmas was over –
With the devil to pay!

And all the best wishes,
And goodwill toward men,
Couldn't bring the Spirit of Christmas
Back once again!

After the Stroke of Midnight

(A Legend)

Although no one knows how it began, there is a legend that all dumb animals are endowed with speech for one hour after midnight on Christmas Eve, in memory of the animals who lingered near the manger when the blessed Christ-child was born (in reward for their silence while the baby Jesus slept in a manger.)

And if their tongues were loosed,
I think this is what they'd say,
As they gather 'round the Christ-child
On that blessed Christmas Day!

"See the newborn baby,
He is the promised King –
God's only begotten Son
Sent forth to reign!"

Bethlehem's star's so brightly shining,
Over where the baby, Jesus, lies,
There is a hush over the little town,
As God's Spirit hovers nigh.

Behold His Mother, Mary,
As they gather 'round that threshold,
The earth is filled with wonder
Of a Christmas all aglow.

Hear the Holy Angels
Announcing the news in the sky,
Rejoicing and praising,
With the Shepherds who tend nearby.

The rocks and rills are ringing,
With Peace and Goodwill toward men,
Proclaiming the glad tidings,
As Heaven's Glory doth descend.

They would speak to one another
In tones so "sweet and low,"
Their hearts would talk of Love,
And God's kindnesses here below.

Yes, we know it's but a "legend,"
But, you know how a legend grows,
Perhaps the Spirit of Christmas is "so great,"
That all of Creation knows!

A Real American Christmas

Christmas is in the air,
Shoppers are seen everywhere.

Lots of gifts we need to buy,
Before Santa and his reindeer fly.

We've got a list, and checked it twice,
We've decided who's naughty or nice.

Although on our gifts, we did splurge,
We couldn't contain ourselves,
 'cause we had the urge.

Long johns for Grandpa,
And an iron skillet for Grandma,

A stuffed critter for little Zeb,
And a pair of new skates for Deb.

These are just to name a few,
Because our list just grew and grew.

Although our colons have gone spastic,
It's all because … this Christmas was "plastic."

Many Happy Returns

Christmas is over –
The presents are in a diminished mound,
I'm so sad and disappointed,
At what I have found.

It seems I already have one of this or that,
And nothing seems to fit,
With gifts too large or too small,
With them I sit.

Later, the sales clerk said to me,
"It states one size fits all –"
"I don't see how that can be," I replied, –
"When some people are short, some tall."

So, somehow, I manage to get a refund,
Though not cheerfully given,
Ready to stand in mile long lines,
Out of necessity I am driven.

It seems to me the gift-givers
Sure are slow to learn,
With a double meaning given to
Merry Christmas and "many happy returns."

The Christmas Gift!

It seemed Christmas had lost its meaning,
Midst all the packages tied up with bow,
I pondered this in my heart,
As I watched the falling snow.

I thought of the busy, bustling shoppers,
Spending more than they had,
How we've commercialized Christmas,
Were the thoughts within my head.

Mistletoe and holly,
Santa Clauses at every mall,
The endless lines and endless lists,
Was Christmas really worth it all?

I thought of jingle bells and snowmen,
And of the usual Christmas cheer,
But, somehow I could not help
But shed a Christmas tear.

Is Christ being left out of Christmas?
As I gazed upon the tree,
All decked with ornaments, tinsel, and lights
For everyone to see.

But, then I espied a package,
That made me once again believe,
As I carefully unwrapped the gift to find,
A replica of the "Blessed Nativity!"

Please Don't

This story is about when I was age seven, and the snowman we built was melting. I knew Mother could do something, and this is my dilemma and how she solved it.

Don't let the snowman melt –
Please never let it go,
Can't Mother do something?
She seems to always know.
The sunshine is so very bright,
And Frosty's slipping fast away,
I try not to cry.
But, tears happen everyday,
"Please, please, Mr. Sun,
If you knew how much fun,
And how he became so very real –
And now you've come –
How can you steal?
He's ours, he is –
And he's melting away each day."
But, Mother said –
"It'll snow again someday,
And you can build another,
We have to have sunshine, too,
Frosty will return again,
Then you won't be so blue,"
And so I wave good-bye,
Trying to believe what grown-ups say –
"Good-bye Frosty – I love you,
Please come again someday."

From "My House" to "Your House"

This warm greeting is filled
With lots of Christmas cheer,
From my house to your house,
To friends afar and to friends near.

As Bethlehem's star shines down on you,
And lights the corner where you are,
May you recount the story of Christmas,
As you follow the wise men from afar.

I bring you tidings of great joy,
Of a Savior born for all,
You'll find the Babe lying in a manger,
As that Holy Night you do recall.

Come, sit a spell by your fireside hearth,
As we take out time to pause,
From our hurried, busy schedules,
In our wait for Santa Claus.

May it be a Christmas bright and merry,
As children gather 'round the tree,
May sleigh rides, snowmen and jingle bells,
Make this holiday scene "complete."

From my house to your house,
I bid you God's peace, "Shalom."
May God's Presence dwell
Within our humble homes.

May you enjoy old friends
Good food and great times,
For there's no better place to be,
Than home at Christmastime.

From my house to your house,
From my heart to yours,
May all the many blessings
Of Christmas be ours!

This Christmas

This Christmas, send Thy Light,
That led the wise men through the night,

Send Thy Peace and Love,
That settle gently as a Dove.

Send Thy Goodwill and Cheer,
May Thy Presence be ever near.

Send Thy Glad Tidings of great joy,
That tell the Story of the "Manger Boy,"

Illuminate the world with Truth and Right,
That lift our souls to Heaven's height.

Place Thy Hope within each heart,
As we worship and praise, "How Great Thou Art!"

And send everything that makes Christmas bright,
And if you should please, Lord,
"Make it white!"

That Holy Night

Let hearts rejoice and voices sing
Of the Advent of our Lord and King!
Proclaim Christ's birth on that Holy Night,
When the Son of God, came to be our light.
Retell the story grown ever so dear,
As hearts to that sacred scene draw near.
On hallowed threshold, gather around,
Where our Hope of peace and joy is found.
Where Bethlehem's Babe in a manger lay –
The Promised King, on a bed of hay.
The Lord over all, born without a crown,
To that lowly stable, humbly stepped down.
Yet, though the world afforded him no place,
Still, "open hearts" may behold His face.
So reverently may hushed whispers fall,
As we breathe "Sweet Jesus – Savior born for all."

All That Christmas Brings

Christmas means so many things:
Happy faces all aglow,
The cheery warmth of an open hearth
Nestled snugly from blanketed snow.
Whispers of Santa's reindeer and sleigh,
Packages bound with ribbon and bow,
The aroma of Mama's Christmas treats,
Trees and lights and mistletoe.
In the midst of this excitement,
I find that I must pause,
As my heart makes its list
In the wait for Santa Claus.
For all of this I am so thankful,
For the love of family and friends,
For all the goodwill, peace and joy
That "Merry Christmas" sends.
But, unto God I am most thankful,
For His Son sent from Above,
For all the blessings of Christmas
Are bound up in His Love.

The Best Present This Christmas

The best present this Christmas,
The best you'll ever find,
Is the Christ-child born in a manger,
Sent in God's fullness of time.

You may give and receive many presents,
But, if Christ lives in your heart,
That's the greatest gift ever received,
For Christ was rent from God's own heart.

For God so loved the world,
He gave us the gift of His Son,
So let God's peace, love, joy and light,
Ring out through all Christendom!

Everyday Should Be Like Christmas

Everyday should be like Christmas,
Three hundred and sixty-five days a year,
Filled with light and hope and joy,
And lots of Christmas cheer.

Everyday should be like Christmas,
With giving and caring and love,
Wrapped in peace and goodwill toward men,
Sent from the Father Above.

Everyday should be like Christmas,
May its spirit live in our hearts,
And even when the season has ended,
May its message never depart.

Doing good unto our fellow man,
Giving thanks unto the Father Above,
These are the things that lift the heart,
And fill our lives with love.

Let's share the Christmas Story,
With everyone we meet,
And spread the glad tidings of the Savior,
Born to make our lives complete.

Yes, everyday should be like Christmas,
In our every thought and way,
So let's take each day and live it
Just like it was "Christmas Day!"

The Wise Ones See a King

Come, gather 'round the manger,
And view that Holy scene,
Some see a only a baby,
But, the wise ones see a King.

Bearing gifts of gold, frankincense and myrrh,
Three wise men traveled from afar,
Being guided by the wondrous light,
Of Bethlehem's beautiful star.

The angels announced "good tidings of great joy"
To shepherds tending their flocks nearby,
"Peace on earth, goodwill toward men,"
Sang the hosts from on high.

Wicked King Herod sought the young child's life,
But, the wise men were warned in a dream,
In the fullness of time, God's plan was fulfilled,
Despite satan's wicked schemes.

The promised Messiah hath come,
Let loud Hosannas ring,
And when you celebrate this Christmas,
Remember this one thing,

While some see a only a baby,
The wise ones see a King.

Christmas Day

On this merry Day of Christmas,
May God's love on us descend,
Lift up our hearts
And make us like children once again.

To see the wonder and the beauty,
Of a Christmas white and bright,
To hear the Holy Angels announce,
The birth of the Savior that holy night.

Let us capture the true meaning
Of a Christmas all aglow,
Midst the jolly time in snow flurry
Midst trees, lights and mistletoe.

May we keep the Spirit of Christmas
In things we do and say,
As we look back upon the manger,
And see the Christ-child where He lay.

Lord Jesus, come live in our hearts,
With peace on earth, goodwill toward men,
In simple faith and trust,
Make us like children once again.

And They Called Him Jesus

He is known as the man of Calvary,
He lived in relative obscurity.
He is the Prince of Peace,
And the Risen Lamb is He.

He is the Promised Messiah,
God with Us – Immanuel.
He is the Son of God,
Sent to save our souls from hell.

He is meek and lowly in heart,
Yet, Lord of Lord's and King of Kings,
May Heaven and earth sing His praises,
Let loud Hosannas ring.

He forsook the splendors of Heaven,
To take away our sin and blame,
He is the Alpha and Omega,
And lives, He still doth change.

The Christ-child was born in Bethlehem,
Sent to heal all our soul's diseases,
He is the Savior to the world,
And He is called Jesus.

The Best Gift

What should I give this Christmas?
As I look at my holiday list,
Would Mary like that, I wonder?
Would Timmy or Johnny like this?

As I sit and contemplate,
All that I have to do,
It seems work is never done,
And the shopping is never through.

Baking each one's favorite treats,
Shuffling in bustling crowds,
With so much left to do,
Sometimes I want to scream aloud.

There's more to Christmas than
Decorated trees and twinkling lights,
Snowmen or holly and mistletoe;
Of the manger we must keep sight.

For God sent His precious Son,
To be our Savior from Above,
And the best gift to give at Christmastime
Is love.

A Picture!

I can paint a picture
With a thousand words,
Or, with a single word,
I can paint a thousand pictures.
Spring!

It's Spring!

It's spring, it's spring!
The leaves are turning green,
There is a Midas touch on everything,
With joy my heart doth sing.

Bees are flitting from flower to flower,
And we anticipate the April showers,
Beauty unfolds each moment of each hour,
Of hanging gardens and lovely bowers.

It's spring, it's spring!
As fresh as the morning dew,
The sun-kissed earth hath come alive,
And everything is born anew.

It's spring, it's spring!
The birds so sweetly sing,
It seems the bells of Heaven are ringing,
Announcing that it's spring.

It's spring, it's spring!
Lovely fragrances fill the air,
And if you will look you will find
That God is everywhere.

Of the four seasons,
Spring, summer, winter and fall,
Spring is the most enthralling,
And is to me, the loveliest of all.

Summertime Fun

Get out your fishing pole,
With winter, we are done,
So kick off your shoes and go barefoot,
Have some summertime fun!

Drink lemonade in the shade,
Go on picnics, too,
Snow cones and baseball games,
There are so many things to do!

Enjoy your vegetable garden,
Which makes food taste gourmet,
Take a siesta when you are through,
And take in some sunny rays.

Sit a spell in your porch swing,
And watch the world go by,
Make homemade ice cream,
The kind that you can't buy!

Sit out under the stars at night,
In the good ol' summertime,
When living is easy and life's at its best,
And doesn't cost a dime!

Hope in Resurrection

Dark gloom encircled that empty tomb,
When, Mary, despondent, with weeping eye,
Turned away, bereft of hope,
Seeing only a gardener nearby.

But, she left that tomb rejoicing,
Renewed in a hope held high,
When she knew 'twas not a gardener
But, the Master standing nigh.

And the disciples told that "stranger"
Whom they supposed new to Galilee,
About their lost hope in the man
Who had just died at Calvary.

With sad and doubting faces,
They told how hope had been undone,
For the Promised King was gone,
Who had claimed to be God's Son.

Continued

But, when they saw with "seeing eyes,"
Smote in the heart were they,
For they knew 'twas not a stranger
They'd entertained that day.

And when the disciples were gathered,
Fearful and lonely in that room,
Jesus came and stood among them
As proof of the empty tomb.

He upbraided their fear and disbelief,
For faith wanting to be found,
For by the power of the Resurrection,
Death could not keep Him in the ground.

When they saw His nail-scarred Hands
And felt His spear-torn Side,
They understood Resurrection's Hope,
For to "raise us up," He died.

Hallelujah! We Shall Rise!

On that glorious Resurrection,
When Jesus comes yonder in the skies,
We shall be changed to be like Him,
Hallelujah! We shall rise!

Raised by God's mighty power,
Nevermore to die,
The graves shall burst asunder,
Hallelujah! We shall rise!

Clothed in Christ's righteousness,
Numbered with the happy and free,
We shall shine as the stars of the firmament,
For throughout Eternity.

The trumpet of God shall sound,
And time shall be no more,
Former things will be passed away,
And we'll meet on that beautiful shore.

Oh, that day of Resurrection,
Under Heaven's unclouded skies,
Won't you be a part of that Great Day,
When hallelujah! We shall rise!

Let's Listen to What the Angels Had to Say!

Oh, what a bright Resurrection morn,
The gravestone was rolled away,
Draw near and let's listen
To what the Angels had to say.

"He is not dead, He is risen,
Come see the place where the Lord lay,"
Hear them proclaim the joyful news –
Of the empty grave!

See Mary, running,
Fearful, trembling at the sight,
As the Cross gleamed in victory,
In the morning light!

Yes, Jesus Christ is living,
And He dwells in hearts today,
He sits at the Father's Right Hand,
And still hears a sinner pray.

He nailed our sins to His Cross,
So we might live in Heaven, someday,
So draw near and let's listen …
To what the Angels had to say!

The Message of an Empty Tomb

The morning light has broken,
And has dispelled night's gloom,
The walls resound with an echo
With a message from an empty tomb.

"He is not here, He is risen,"
Faith at last has found room,
The gravestone is rolled away,
And Jesus will come back again soon.

Christ came to bring us hope,
To save us from hell's doom,
The earth shook, the rocks rent,
And left an empty tomb.

And here in my heart,
The Rose of Sharon forever blooms,
For that is the message
Of the "empty tomb!"

First Light

The Cross stood in silhouette
Against the morning sky,
For three days Jesus had lain in the grave,
For our sins He was crucified.

Mary and other women came early to the sepluchre,
The great gravestone was rolled away,
"He is not here, He is Risen,"
They heard the Angel say.

But, they left that tomb rejoicing
Renewed in a hope held high,
Clouds of gloom were dispelled,
As Mary saw the Savior standing nigh.

Praise God! We serve a risen Savior,
He did not lose the fight,
For the world was changed forever,
That morning at "first light!"

Victory's Hour

Death could not claim Him,
The grave could not keep Him,
The Resurrection proclaimed Him,
Oh, won't you receive Him?

Come, take an Easter pilgrimage,
See the place where Jesus lay,
See the linen grave clothes,
See how the stone was rolled away!

Seek Him among the living,
Find Him in Truth and Love and Joy,
He saves the lost and dying soul,
So nothing can destroy.

Some glad day the saved will be raised,
To meet Him in the air,
No more tears nor partings,
No more of life's burdens or care.

"He is not here," the Angel proclaimed,
"He is Risen," in Resurrection's Power,
The morning light broke through the night
And gleamed in victory's hour!

He's Alive!

They crucified our Savior,
At Calvary, He died,
But, He arose on the third day,
And today, He is alive!

If you wonder why Jesus came,
God's great Love was why,
So shout it from the mountaintops,
He's alive!

They said His body was stolen,
But, that was satan's lie,
By God's Power of Resurrection,
He's alive!

Someday, He will come again,
So dry your weeping eyes,
In great Power and Glory,
For He's alive!

With the Saints and Holy Angels,
He'll roll back the skies,
"All things will confess His Name,"
That He's alive!

Throughout the Eternal Ages,
We'll sing from on High,
"Glory be unto God,"
He's alive, He's alive!

Mary in the Morning

There's nothing quite so wonderful
As seeing Mary in the morning,
Coming to the empty tomb,
With hope the world adorning.

There was a great earthquake,
The gravestone was rolled away,
"He is not here; He is risen,"
Mary heard the Angel say.

Early and eagerly seeking Jesus,
To anoint with sweet perfume,
Her heart was filled with joy,
For God's love was in full bloom.

While the world lay asleep,
Draped in the blackness of mourning,
God's promise was being fulfilled,
In the dawn of Easter morning.

Mary left that tomb rejoicing,
Knowing the Savior came to die,
Just so that on the third day,
Victoriously He would arise!

Righteousness and Truth kissed
In that morning light,
Seeing Mary in the morning,
Sets the whole world aright.

Someday

Someday, I'm going to sail
Right past the moon and sun and stars,
And hitch a ride on the Milky Way,
I'll fly high and far.

My troubles will all be over,
I'll tell this world good-bye,
I'll live in perfect peace and joy
In that sweet bye and bye.

So when you hear I have gone,
On this truth you can rely,
I am living in my Heavenly home,
Where my soul shall never die.

I Will Work For Jesus 'Till He Comes

I will work for Jesus 'till He comes,
I will work from dawn 'till setting sun,
I will pray His Kingdom will soon come,
I will work for Jesus 'till He comes.

I will tell the lost of Jesus,
I will win them one by one,
I'll work and watch and pray,
Until the whole world be won.

I will live to see Him smile,
I'll do those things worthwhile,
So that when I've walked life's final mile,
I will hear Him say "Well done."

All For the Love of Lost Souls

All for the sea of humanity,
All for the love of lost souls,
Jesus lay down His life at Calvary,
Leaving Heaven's riches untold.

He loosed the chains of sin,
For His grace sets us free,
He left Heaven's ivory palaces,
To come for you and for me.

"For God so loved the world,
He gave His only begotten Son,
That whosever believeth in Him …"
Shall have a Heaven in the world to come.

He cared for our eternal destiny,
His touch doth make us whole,
All for the sea of humanity,
All for the love of lost souls.

The Value of a Soul

Jesus left His Throne in Heaven,
And to Calvary did go,
To show us God's great love,
And the value of a soul.

Nails pierced His Hands and Feet,
In agony tossed his soul,
At Calvary, love was put to the test,
That's the value of a soul.

Won't you trust Jesus to save,
His touch can make you whole,
It took Jesus' death to save just one,
That's the value God placed on a soul.

No one can ever understand it all,
Just why God loved us so,
But, we know one thing for certain,
That's the value of a soul.

Far Away From The Streets of Gold

If you live for this life only,
And take no thought for your lost soul,
Someday, your life will be empty,
Far away from the streets of gold.

Far away from those pearly gates,
And those beautiful mansions untold,
Far away from that City so white,
Where no one ever grows old.

Yield your stubborn will today,
God's saving grace to know,
Or you'll be separated from the love of God,
Far away from the streets of gold.

You'll miss all the things you hold dear,
All the happiness you could know,
If you fail to trust in Jesus
You'll spend Eternity in hell below.

Don't wait until it's too late to be saved,
Let Christ's touch make you whole,
Else tomorrow may mean that you will be,
Far away from the streets of gold.

Yesterday Again

People say yesterday is gone,
But, don't listen to what they say,
We'll all meet yesterday again
In the Judgment Day.

The Great White Throne Judgment,
Is where the lost will stand,
For the sin of unbelief in Jesus,
They'll miss Heaven's Golden Strand.

The Judgment Seat of Christ,
Is where all the saved shall stand,
But, the blood of lost souls
Will be required at their hand.

It is not a pretty picture,
But, it doesn't have to be this way,
We still have time to repent
While God grants yet another day.

What will we do with Jesus?
Is the great question of the soul,
Will you be safe in the Arms of Jesus
While the eternal Ages roll?

For one thing is certain,
On this you can depend,
When we see Jesus face to Face,
We'll all meet up with yesterday again.

Is This World a Better Place?

Is the world a better place
Because of me?
Have I been a positive influence,
My life, a living testimony?

Does my light so shine
In this darkened world,
That it reflects Jesus
With God's banner of love unfurled?

When I leave this world, someday,
Will it be a little brighter, a little kinder, too?
Will someone receive a blessing,
Because of something that I do?

Will the good that I have done,
Somewhere fill a need,
In the lives that touch mine,
Will I scatter precious seed?

Did I tell the lost of Jesus?
Did I point to them, God's saving grace?
For someday, I feel I'll have to answer,
Did I make this world a better place?

A Sad, Sad Day

When the unsaved stand in the Judgment,
Called the Great White Throne,
It will be a sad, sad day,
To not be one of Christ's own.

All the allure of this world,
Will then hold no sway,
Forever separated from the love of God,
It will be a sad, sad day.

Oh, to be lost and undone,
When God calls your name,
And then there'll be no one else,
But, yourself to blame.

But, what you would then give
In exchange for your soul,
To have forfeited saving grace,
That could have made you whole.

"Depart from Me, I never knew you,"
Are the words you'll hear Jesus say,
As you'll think about "what might have been –"
'Twill be a sad, sad day.

All hope will then be gone,
And not left, even a single ray,
All because of unbelief in Jesus,
Oh, it will be a sad, sad day.

Somebody Needs Jesus Today

Somebody is out there,
On the dark hills astray,
Somebody needs someone
To point unto them the way.

Somebody needs to be lifted,
Above life's fray,
Somebody is hurting,
Somebody needs Jesus today.

Somebody needs someone
O'er their souls to pray,
Who'll reach to help them,
As they travel life's way.

Somebody is lonely,
In need of Jesus, the Friend,
Who'll walk with them
Unto journey's end.

Somebody is waiting,
For you to show them the way,
Don't betray their trust,
Because somebody needs Jesus today.

Someday, May Be One Day Too Late

Someday, you plan to be saved,
But, friend why do you wait?
Tomorrow may never come,
And, someday, may be one day too late.

It appointed unto man once to die,
After this the Judgment Day,
The unsaved will stand at the Great White Throne,
So soon will come that someday.

The devil wants to keep you from Heaven,
In hell, he wants to seal your fate,
Answer while Jesus is knocking,
Someday, may be one day too late.

Don't you want to go to Heaven,
And pass through those pearly gates?
Today is the day of Salvation,
For someday, may be one day … too late.

One By One

Win the world to Jesus,
Win them one by one,
Labor for the Master,
From dawn 'till setting sun.

Do your duty, never falter,
'Till a Heavenly crown be won,
Tell them on the highways and byways,
Bid the lost to Jesus come.

Win the world to Jesus,
Win them one by one,
Until you pass through those pearly gates,
And you hear God say "Well done."

Work for the night is falling,
Work 'till God's kingdom come,
Win the world to Jesus,
Win them one by one.

"What Could Have Been"

Do you have a minute, my friend?
I have something I want to share,
It's the Good News of the Gospel,
About Jesus who truly cares.

Of how He came to save you,
And to forgive you of your sins,
Of how He went to Calvary,
And how He's coming back again.

Of how He's prepared mansions for us,
In Heaven's home Above,
For all who've trusted Him as Savior,
In the free pardon of His Love.

My heart is breaking for you,
If you've never accepted His grace,
For, someday, He will be your Judge,
And you'll meet Him face to Face.

We have no promise of tomorrow,
God alone sees around the bend,
But, the saddest words ever penned,
Are the words, "what could have been."

Today is the day of Salvation,
Ask Christ into your heart,
For in hell you will bewail your Fate,
And of God's Grace, have no part.

The Saints are gathering over Yonder,
On that happy golden shore,
Won't you join that bright number,
And be safe forevermore?

I Want To Share Heaven With You

I want to share Heaven with you,
To tell you about what Jesus can do,
He's the Friend who is Faithful and True,
Who can give you life anew.

I want to share Heaven with you,
In that land beyond the blue,
I want to share the Good News of the Gospel,
So you can go there, too!

So that we will meet again,
In that land of golden tomorrows,
Where all is peace and joy and love,
And we'll never know another sorrow.

Jesus for our sins once died,
At Calvary, He paid the cost,
To redeem fallen mankind,
To save souls so lost.

So that we could go to a home over yonder,
When this life is through,
And live with Jesus forever and ever,
Oh, how, I want to share Heaven with you.

The Brink of Eternity

We're standing on the brink of Eternity,
Not knowing what a day may hold,
Multitudes are facing the decision,
Regarding the state of their souls.

But, God proffers His saving grace,
It's the greatest love story ever told,
Because of Jesus' sacrifice at Calvary,
We can walk on Heaven's "streets of gold."

O' soul without a Savior,
Won't you believe upon Christ today?
For we're standing on the brink of Eternity,
And we're only one heartbeat away.

We Only Say "Good-bye" So We Can Say "Hello"

Jesus is the Friend who never fails,
He directs where our footsteps go,
And tells us we only have to say "good-bye"
Just so we can say "hello."

He's got our dear loved ones,
Safely within His care,
And no ill winds ever blow
Under Heaven's skies so fair.

And He will not ask of us,
Above what we can bear,
He feels our every sorrow,
And our heartaches, He doth share.

Even when we pass ol' Jordan,
Through which we must go,
We'll know we only say "good-bye,"
Just so we can say "hello."

So remember that after that sad "goodbye"
Soon comes that "first hello,"
Heaven is only a prayer away,
Don't miss those streets of gold.

So together we shall praise Him,
As the eternal ages roll,
As the Master of our lives
And the Savior of our souls.

A Home Beyond the River

I've a home beyond the river,
Where the streets are paved with gold,
I'll live in a beautiful mansion,
And no one will ever grow old.

Disappointments will never come,
And there'll be no tear-dimmed eyes,
There'll be no more sickness or pain,
And no more sad good-byes.

The flowers there will be blooming,
In that garden of Paradise,
Where there is peace and sweet rest,
Under Heaven's unclouded skies.

I've a home beyond the river,
Where life is made complete,
Where all is joy and love,
And the victory is sweet.

In that home beyond the river,
Time shall be no more,
Loved ones will be waiting to welcome me,
Upon that golden shore.

Oh, I've a home beyond the river,
Known as that "sweet bye and bye,"
Where we shall live forever with Jesus
And our souls shall never die.

Someday, I'll Wake Up in Heaven

Someday, I'll wake up in Heaven,
All earth's troubles will be o'er,
Loved ones will be waiting to greet me,
Upon that fair and golden shore.

Someday, I'll wake up in Heaven,
Life's dark night will be past,
I'll enter the portals of Glory
And finally be home at last.

Heaven's bells will be peeling,
In melodious and rapturous song,
And we'll praise our dear Savior,
Forever on and on.

Jesus will be there to welcome us,
As we pass through those pearly gates,
In ecstasy we shall stroll
Over Heaven's vast estate.

Someday, the saved will wake up in Heaven,
All our battles will be through,
We shall shine as the stars forever,
And all things will be new.

Another Meeting Place

Here, we know tears of sorrow,
And oft it's so hard to say good-bye,
But, there's another meeting place
Up yonder in the sky.

Where we'll join hands again,
In that fair, unending day,
Trials will all be over,
And joy will come to stay.

Nothing can ever harm us,
Sin cannot hold sway,
There'll be no partings, ever,
And on golden harps we'll play.

We'll walk on streets of gold,
And join in Heaven's glad song,
No more heartaches or disappointments,
For all our troubles will be gone.

No more worries o'er the future,
For our lives will be bright and gay,
We'll sit at the Master's Feet,
And learn of all He has to say.

And we'll never look back to earthly things,
For former things shall be passed away,
Forgotten will be life's ills and woes,
As troubled waters that passed our way.

Yes, there's another meeting place,
Where we'll be gathered together for aye,
There's another meeting place,
Where the skies are never gray.

Where there will be no more sadness,
For we'll see Jesus face to Face,
Oh, Praise God, when this life is over,
That there is another meeting place!

Where Teardrops Never Fall

Here on earth we have troubles,
Many evils do befall,
But, I'm going to a land of golden tomorrows
Where teardrops never fall.

Here, we have our sorrows,
And crosses we must bear,
And often we must say good-bye
To things we hold so dear.

But, in Heaven, loved ones will be waiting,
With open arms to welcome us home,
And we'll live in bliss forever,
Singing praises around God's Throne.

Oh, what a glad day is coming,
To all who have believed
Accepting Christ as their personal Savior,
His saving grace to have received.

Our "Glory, Glory Hallelujah's,"
Will echo throughout Eternity's halls,
No more sin to destroy,
And no teardrops to ever fall.

I'll Be Shouting "Glory!"

I'll be shouting "Glory!"
As the eternal ages roll,
I'll be kickin' up gold dust
Upon those streets of gold.

I'll be praising Jesus,
And be safe within God's fold,
I'll be dwelling in beautiful mansions,
Where the half has not yet been told.

I'll be shouting "Glory!"
Nevermore to grow old,
No more troubles or trials,
No heartaches there like here below.

I'll be shouting "Glory!"
Let the Hallelujahs roll,
For I'm on my way to Heaven,
Where only fair winds blow.

And I will claim sweet victory,
In triumph o'er the foe,
And retell that sweet Old Story,
About the Savior of my soul.

That Will Be Heaven To Me!

Just to see our dear loved ones
Gathered just over the Crystal Sea,
Just one touch of their dear hand,
Oh, that will be Heaven to me!

Just a glimpse of my dear Savior,
Just to sit at His Feet,
Just one sight of those mansions of Glory,
Oh, that will be Heaven to me!

Just one rose that blooms in Paradise,
On and on throughout Eternity,
Just one pearl at the gates of Glory,
Oh, that will be Heaven to me!

Just one voice of a Heavenly angel,
Just one word from the Father of Lights,
Just one note from the Heavenly choir,
Just one "Hello" will make everything right!

Just to hear my name once called
On the "roll call" over yonder,
To be crowned with the faithful and true,
'Twill be all my heart can ponder.

Just to remember Calvary's cross,
And know my sin's are gone,
By the blood of Jesus, the Lamb,
And now Heaven is my home ...

Just to dwell in His Holy Presence,
And bow before God's Throne,
Where everyone in Heaven knows my name.
Just to be known as I am known.

Just one view of that pearly white City,
Just one step upon those golden streets,
Just one voice of praise from the Redeemed ones,
Oh, that will be Heaven to me!

Just to sit a spell by the River,
And talk to Jesus about Calvary,
Just one sight of that dear homeland,
Oh, that will be Heaven to me!

Looking in on Paradise

Come with me to the gate,
Let's look in on Paradise,
Jesus is with them there,
He's wiped the tears from their eyes.

You will find our loved ones there,
In that garden oh, so fair,
Nary a worry or care,
Never a burden to bear.

In Heaven's unclouded skies,
God has explained the reasons why,
No more weary sighs,
There the soul shall never die.

They are sitting at Jesus' Feet,
And their victory is sweet,
They are souls set free,
Never to taste defeat.

Someday, we shall meet them there,
And that meeting will be sweet,
We'll pass through those garden gates,
And our joy will be complete.

Our souls will rise in ecstasy,
As we meet our Savior in the air,
And the holy Angels will bear us home,
To Canaan's land so fair.

Gone But Come

When life's sun is sinking low,
And when life's race is run,
From this life they will be gone,
But, in the next, they will have just come.

Saints and Angels will be rejoicing,
That God's child has come home,
Ready to meet one's rewards,
And reap the harvest that's been sown.

For them, we weep tears of sorrow,
But, we can be comforted to know,
The redeemed dwell in the Presence of Jesus,
No more troubles like here below.

There'll be a grand homecoming,
On life's other side,
When we say they have departed,
They've just crossed that Great Divide.

A royal welcome awaits them,
Where life's victory will be won,
And although we say they've "gone,"
In Heaven, they will "have come."

I've a Longing for Home

I'm getting homesick for Heaven,
For I've had a longing for home,
Ever since the day that Jesus saved me,
When His blood my sins atoned.

I've been anxious to see those mansions,
And to walk on those streets of gold,
To dwell in that pearly white City,
Where we'll nevermore grow old.

A longing to be with my departed loved ones,
And to talk with Saints of Old,
To behold all the wondrous sights,
Where the half has not yet been told.

I've a longing to see Jesus,
The Savior of my soul.
And to sing His praises,
While the ceaseless ages roll.

Yes, I'm getting homesick for Heaven,
Where our cares will be all gone,
For nothing here quite satisfies,
Like the lights of that fair home.

No Strangers in Heaven

There'll be no strangers in Heaven,
We'll feel right at home,
We'll lay life's crosses down
Beneath God's righteous Throne.

It will all be so wonderful,
After earth's trials and tests,
At the end of life's dusty road,
To alas, find peace and rest.

We'll talk with Abraham, Isaac, and Jacob,
And all those Saints of old,
We'll be known as we are known,
And dwell safely within God's fold.

We'll know each other better,
In that day without an end,
We'll sing praises unto Jesus,
Our very dearest Friend.

It will be so good to be home,
Yonder in Heaven so fair,
There'll be no strangers in Heaven,
No, there'll be no strangers there.

We'll live in perfect peace,
In God's light and joy and love,
For nothing here can compare
To the ties we'll have up above.

Yes, we'll know everybody,
And everybody will know us, too,
Accept Christ who died for your sins,
And Heaven will be awaiting you.

Everyday

Everyday, there is a fight for freedom,
Everyday a battle cry,
For the price of liberty
Runs so very high.

To keep Old Glory waving,
Over a free and prosperous land,
Takes men of courage and valor,
Who for right do take a stand.

So everyday I count my blessings,
For so fortunate am I,
Let me never hold my freedom lightly,
When good men are willing to die.

God's Country

This is God's country,
The grand ol' USA
Where I've put down my roots,
And where I plan to stay.

Where air is fresh and clean,
And Old Glory proudly waves,
Where we want to raise our children,
Home to the free and brave.

Where we worship as we please,
And hold our heads up high,
Where we walk tall and proud
Under its starry skies.

Where we tell our tales,
To the generations that follow,
Where we live in hope,
With courage to face tomorrow.

Where you feel like somebody,
Where you meet heroes on the street –
Where life is good –
And where our joys are sweet.

Continued

This is God's Country
Where dreams really do come true –
Where we love our fellow man
As the Good Book tells us to.

Where we sing "The Star Spangled Banner,"
And tears well up in our eyes,
Where our motto is "in God we trust"
And our spirit is "do or die."

Where God's banner of love waves over us,
In this great land of opportunity,
Where if someone falls we lift them up,
Where we never know unless we try.

Where our ideals and values,
Are passed down to the next generation,
Where we uphold the family
And cling to its traditions.

With its majestic mountains,
And fields of golden grain,
Where there is a "horn of plenty,"
Across the hills and plains.

Where our National Bird is the Eagle,
Because he flies high and free,
Symbolic of God's country—
For there's no place I'd rather be.

We are the Sons and Daughters

We are the sons and daughters
Of "sweet liberty,"
Fighting on the front lines,
For homeland security.

We raise Old Glory to the sky,
Never to touch the dust,
And our "motto" still remains,
"In God we trust."

We are a people
Who are proud and strong,
And unto the future generations
Let us pass the torch along.

Our fight is to the finish,
In situations do or die,
But, with the wings of an eagle,
We fly far and high.

We have a rich heritage,
Forefathers who stood for right,
We believe all men are created equal,
In God's blessed sight.

May God's banner of love be over us,
And we sweep from victory to victory,
For we are the sons and daughters
Of "sweet liberty."

As American as "Apple Pie"

When I see "Old Glory" waving proudly,
It brings tears to my eyes,
I wear my heart on my sleeve,
For I'm as American as "apple pie."

When I think of all the sacrifice,
In situations do or die,
I thank the good Lord up Above,
That so richly blessed am I!

For I'm enjoying "sweet liberty,"
And that flag is flying high,
Because someone, somewhere
Was willing to pay the price.

So if you ever question,
Just how deep these roots go,
I'll just say that this American thing,
Tends to only grow and grow.

So, I honor all our military,
And salute the stars and stripes,
Because in my heart I know we're all
As American as "apple pie."

Happy Birthday, America!

For Independence Day, 2010

Happy birthday, America,
Happy birthday to you,
We celebrate our freedom on this day,
And salute the red-white-and blue.

All hail to the stars and stripes,
Long may she ever wave,
One Nation, under God,
Home to the free and the brave.

May freedom's bells keep peeling
The anthem of the free,
And may your big heart keep beating out,
The song of "sweet liberty."

America, you're 234 years young, today,
And no matter what some may say,
The best country in the whole wide world,
Is still the good ol' USA!

May God preserve and defend Thee,
And may your skies always be blue,
Happy birthday, America,
Happy birthday to you!

One More Person Strong

When you cast your vote in this election,
And help to right the wrong,
You'll make America stronger,
One more person strong.

Sing it loud and clear,
The glory of freedom's song,
Help to make America stronger,
One more person strong.

Don't wait until our liberties,
Are all taken away,
It's up to each of us,
It's time to stand up without delay.

You may ask yourself the question,
Just what can one person do?
But, you are in the majority
When it's God and you.

It's time to be counted,
In this great country to which we belong,
So help make this country stronger,
One more person strong.

I'm Happy to be an American

I'm happy to call myself an American,
Home to the brave and free,
And to see Old Glory waving
Proudly and stately in the breeze.

From the President to the pauper,
Each has equality,
And I can call this land mine,
As far as my eyes can see.

To be a part of the Great Melting Pot,
Where each has individuality,
I'm glad that in its great big heart,
It found room enough for me.

From the black gold of Texas,
To the hills of Tennessee,
To the Redwoods of California,
It will always be "home" to me.

Heroes Seldom Say

They fought for our liberty,
A great price they had to pay,
Willingly they sacrificed,
Although heroes "seldom say."

We owe them our gratitude,
Our loyalty and our prayers,
They need to know they're not forgotten,
And that somebody cares.

They don't talk much about war,
They live with their memories,
They had a job to do, and did it,
So that we might be free.

But, we know our flag flies high today,
Because they paved the way,
Let's let them know what it means to us,
Because heroes "seldom say."

America

Don't wait until troubles come,
And bring us to our knees,
Cast your vote for right,
Lead us on to victory.

May God bless America,
Long may Old Glory wave,
May God's favor be upon us,
Home of the true and brave.

Cling to our motto,
"In God we trust,"
And leave behind a legacy,
Untouched by moth or rust.

May love's banner be over us,
May it always be this way,
And may we feel a national pride,
As we hear our anthem play.

You may think it doesn't matter,
That we can do as we please,
Don't wait for a wake-up call,
That brings us to our knees.

May God preserve our nation,
May we always we free,
And lift our voices to proclaim,
"Long live sweet liberty!"

A Tribute to Our Servicemen

Forgive us when we take for granted,
Our freedom that is so dear –
Or fail to heed the sacrifice or cost –
Or fail to shed a tear.
May hearts be filled with gratitude –
For deeds, both great and small,
For battles fought, for struggles,
For heroes, one and all.
Because of you, our children
May never march to war,
Let hearts unite and may Veterans
Always find an open door.
May that multitude of faces
Journey with us everyday –
Those who trod a rugged path
That they might pave the way.
May our lives never become shallow –
May emotions never run dry,
Where lives were sacrificed
In the fight for freedom's cry.
God bless our servicemen
Who gallantly took a stand,
To keep Old Glory waving
Over a free and prosperous land!

A True American Hero

Dedicated to my Dad, Carl W. Hixon on a Father's Day

You enlisted in the Army,
Fighting in the Second World War,
You are a bigger than life hero,
They just don't make them like you anymore.

Because of you, many have found refuge,
Upon our fair shore,
You can hold your head up high,
For they just don't make them like you anymore.

Wounded and weary, you came home,
And overhead waved the red-white and blue,
You said it was your duty to serve,
But, our freedom depended on you.

So we salute you –
An American to the core,
Who paved the way for liberty,
They just don't make them like you anymore.

For when the Lord made you,
He then broke the mold,
You are a true-blue American,
With a heart of pure gold.

And so on this Father's Day,
Your heroism speaks aloud,
Just to think that you're my Dad,
Sure does make me proud!

A "Salute"

Dedicated to my Dad, Carl W. Hixon, on Veteran's Day

May your sacrifice not be forgotten,
May your memory live on,
A soldier sent off to war,
So we might sing freedom's song.

Among men, you stand tall,
And, as Americans, we stand proud,
So we "salute" you on this day,
For you're head and shoulders above the crowd.

We bow our heads and say a prayer,
For other soldiers who fought like you,
Who deserve a special tribute,
For defending the red-white-and blue.

Some did not return home,
Their sacrifice, their lives,
Leaving behind family and friends,
Their courage cannot be denied.

In the thick of the conflict,
Waging as World War II,
You were a comrade — a brother,
And our freedom depended upon you.

We want to express our gratitude,
For our hearts are very full,
Yet, despite the great price you paid,
Love of country had the greater pull.

Our "hats go off" to you today,
You were there when it counted most,
You're rewards are stored up in Heaven,
With freedom here to host.

So, for all the good you've done,
You have this legacy to show,
This great free land of realized dreams …
You're a bigger than life "hero!"

Old Glory

"Old Glory" tells a story,
Its red-white-and-blue,
Tells a tale of heroes
Whose patriotism rings true!

The stripes of red symbolize the blood,
That it cost to keep us free,
The stars proclaim the brotherhood
Of our great Unity.

The number of the stripes –
Represent the first thirteen states,
United by a common cause,
Woven with love instead of hate.

We feel a pride words can't describe,
Each time she proudly waves,
And we brush away a tear,
For that flag has much to say.

Founded on God's principles,
Long may she ever wave,
One Nation, under God, indivisible,
Home to the free and the brave!

The Price of Liberty

Dedicated to my Dad, Carl W. Hixon, a Veteran of World War II.

He was a soldier sent off to battle,
Sacrificing for you and me,
All for love of country,
And that of "sweet liberty."

Great was the responsibility,
He was called upon to bear,
Yet, duty came foremost,
And heard was his Mother's prayer.

For he came back safely,
Wounded, weary and worn,
Many soldiers did not return,
But, they say that "is war."

He held the flag up high,
Never did it touch the dust,
Knowing the freedom for which we stand,
Depended upon "in God we trust."

Continued

Strong runs our patriotism,
As pride wells in out hearts,
And we watch Old Glory proudly wave,
And we're made to feel a part.

With courage and valor,
Of great acts of bravery,
And a hero's welcome home,
"Trailing clouds" of victory.

And so with thankful hearts,
Today, our heads are reverently bowed,
In service to our country,
You have made us proud.

By the grace of God, and at a great price,
We can now go free,
All for love of country,
And that of "sweet liberty."

The Story of the Eagle

Did you know that when the mighty eagle molts,
He is not alone?
His fellow helpmates come to his rescue,
To make their presence known.

They urge him to not give up,
But to keep in the fight,
They swoop down and call to him,
To make sure he's all right.

As they urge him on,
They supply his every need,
This is the stuff that life is made of,
Their message seems to plead.

And when he answers back,
Though the struggle be at length,
Because they care so much,
He gains a newfound strength.

Perhaps you, too are going through,
Something that calls for strength within,
Remember that when the mighty eagle falls,
It's a beginning not an end.

Your friends won't let you call it quits,
It is a situation that's "do or die,"
So when the challenge rises to meet you,
Remember the eagle who once again will fly!

The Eagle and the Storm

Did you know the majestic eagle
Never flies through the storm?
Neither does he wait it out,
Valuable lessons we should learn.

Instead, he flies above the storm,
Rising higher and higher,
With a great show of power,
With wings that never seem to tire.

So, as we run the Christian race,
Keep the eagle foremost in mind,
Even in the midst of storms,
We can know God's peace sublime.

Flying above the storm,
The eagle never is harmed at all,
And with God's grace we can surmount,
Life's troubles, one and all.

Those that wait upon the Lord shall renew their strength,
Mounting up with eagle's wings,
That is God's promise,
To which we may cling.

They shall run and not be weary,
Walk and not faint,
Oh, what a lovely picture
Isaiah 40:31 paints!

The Seagull

Why is it the seagull
Flies out to sea to die?
I wonder the reason,
But, only God knows why.
Could it be a lifetime
Lived so close to land
Needs a final resting place
Free from life's demand?
Perhaps that final flight
Over the breezy, salty sea,
Is the flight of freedom,
The spirit to be free.
How bittersweet must be that final flight
Over the glassy waters,
'Till daylight fades to night.
Maybe it is a message
God left for you and me,
For each must make that final flight
Over the glassy sea.

God's Wonders

God writes the music of the songbird's trill,
He clothes the lilies, oh, so fair,
He watches over the tiny sparrow,
And on our heads, numbers every hair.

He makes the morning stars sing together,
He made the Heavens on vast display,
He paints a rainbow after every storm,
And puts the "extraordinary" into ordinary days.

He keeps a book of remembrance
Of those that speak oft of His Name,
He records our tears, puts them in a bottle,
And sympathizes with our every pain.

His thoughts toward us,
Are more that the sands of the sea,
But, the greatest wonder of them all,
Is God's love for us, on the "Cross of Calvary."

The Summer That Wasn't

In Arkansas, this was the summer that wasn't,
We've skipped from spring to fall,
Record lows—unseasonably cool,
We've had no summer a'tall.

This was the summer that wasn't,
Our gardens didn't grow,
For all our toil and trouble,
We have nothing good to show.

It has rained cats and dogs,
And spoiled our summertime fun,
Yes, this was the summer that wasn't
That we'll remember for years to come!

Summer 2009

The Quietest Room in Town

It is the quietest room in town,
A little old woman sits all alone,
Her hair is silver-white,
She is friendless and unknown.

But, she is patiently waiting,
For the grandest moment of her life,
Heaven's chariots will be coming,
To free her from heartache and strife.

She trusted Jesus as her Savior,
When she was just a little girl,
And she's tried to faithfully serve Christ,
All her days in this ol' world.

A host of angels will gather 'round,
To carry her safely home,
She'll receive a royal welcome,
For in Heaven her name is known.

And though no visitors ever call,
And her phone never rings,
Jesus is her constant Friend,
And she listens to hear the Angels sing.

She knows the day is soon coming,
She doesn't know just when,
But, she's looking forward to the trip,
And that Glory that shall never dim.

There she'll live in mansions,
Her silver-white hair will turn to gold,
And she will dwell in perfect peace,
And nevermore grow old.

The "quietest" room in town, you say?
Friend, how you misunderstand,
A blessed Saint of God is getting ready,
To claim the "Promised Land!"

Winter's Dread

About the pandemic H1N1(Swine Flu) the Fall and Winter of 2009-2010

We religiously use Germ-X,
We do all that we can do,
We buy bacterial fighting hand soap,
And try every advertisement that is new.

We cover our mouth,
When we cough or sneeze,
And avoid the crowds –
Afraid H1N1 germs will do as they please.

We open the doorknob with our hanky,
And use our elbow to turn on the light,
We prop the door with our knee,
Something about this picture isn't right!

And although we get our flu shots,
As scheduled on time,
It all still leaves us
With little peace of mind.

Keeping up this first line of defense,
Is like trying to turn back the tide,
For the flu season is upon us,
And there's no place to hide.

We disinfect with very swipe,
Yet, when our daily ritual is through,
Lo and behold, we find,
We've somehow caught the "swine" flu!

Maybe the hog is getting a bad rap,
I don't really know for sure,
I just know that, this too, shall pass,
Meanwhile, we "must endure."

By Way of a Limousine

They'll call it a hearse
And say I'm dead and gone,
But, I'm just going to Heaven in a limousine,
And they are oh, so wrong!

Better than a fancy Lincoln or Cadillac,
So friend, mind what you say,
When they take me down that cemetery road,
To lay me in the grave.

I'm not dead but living,
And would not choose to come back if I could,
A royal welcome in Heaven I'll receive,
So I don't want to be misunderstood.

When you see that funeral procession,
All draped in somber black and gray,
Remember I'm seeing the rainbow's spectrum,
On vast display.

They'll dress me in finery,
And yet, call my clothing a shroud,
But, I'll be clothed in His righteousness,
In a white robe and crown!

And thank you all for all the flowers,
That you might send my way,
But I'm headed to a land,
Where the roses never fade.

Death is not a grim monster,
For the picture is not as it seems,
For I'm only headed to my eternal home
By the way of a limousine.

So remember when you are saying
Your final farewells to me,
I'm on the road to Heaven
In a big fine limousine.

So do not mourn sore as a dove,
For death will only be a dream,
I'm on my way past the Milky Way
In a big black limousine.

In truth, you know I do but jest,
For I'll not be there a' tall.
Your dearly beloved was gently carried by Angels
Into "Eternity's sacred Halls."

Just a Mom

They say I'm "just a mom,"
Who makes those good ol' apple pies,
Who mends scraped knees,
And crosses homework t's and dots the i's.
Who kisses away the hurt,
And makes a child's problems seem but small,
Who is both doctor and nurse,
And is 24/7 on call!
But, there's no job so rewarding,
Though credit is often overdue,
As knowing you've made a difference,
In a life God's entrusted to you.
And although I'm "just a mom,"
Who makes those good ol' apple pies,
I look for proof of my success
Within my children's eyes.

We Watch Them Go

This poem was dedicated to my parents, Carl and Maxine Hixon on their sixty-first Wedding Anniversary.

We watch them when life was young,
As they walk hand in hand,
Carefree, frolicking in the sun,
With the whole world in their hand.

We watch them as they raise their children right,
And, by faith, weather many of life's storms,
We watch them shine a guiding light,
And our hearts are ever warmed.

We watch them in their golden years,
With sweet memories to cling,
Roots run deep and love remains strong,
As they do not fear what tomorrow will bring.

We watch them when their hair has turned silver-gray,
He stops for her and waits,
And together they walk hand in hand,
Through life's garden's gate.

Don't Bring Your Germs to Church

If you are really sick,
With a fever in the lurch,
Use this rule of thumb …
Don't bring your "germs" to church!

God doesn't expect you to come,
And spread your sickness all around,
And I think that this advice
Is Biblically sound.

And, yet there are many sick,
Who insist on giving you "a hug,"
Even though they are contagious
And you might catch their "bug."

For you only disturb the congregation
As your cough drops you unwrap,
And think you go unnoticed …
When the medicines fill your lap.

Seems it would be more Godly
To kill cockroaches at home,
Than to come infect a crowd,
Just to make your presence known.

Then it takes us all forever
To put us back in "the pink,"
So wait until your well,
And your health's again "in sync."

I'm not talking of lame excuses
Used to not fill a church pew,
To stay home at a whim,
Conjured up "out of the blue."

But for honest-to-goodness sickness,
Give your heart a search,
'Cause someone will have to pay
When you bring your "germs" to church!

A Mother's Prayer

What burdens have been lifted,
What crosses and what care,
All because of a mother's love,
All because of a mother's prayer.

How many daybreaks,
After life's dark night,
Hope on the horizon to see,
With life's victory in sight.

Because she sends her petitions,
Right to God's very Throne,
How many sons and daughters,
Have found their way back home.

If life's curtain could be lifted,
I think that we would see,
A bridge of prayers into the gates of Heaven,
That span eternity.

For a mother's prayer will reach
Where no one else would ever dare,
Oh, the things that have been wrought
By a mother's prayer.

Because of Somebody's Prayer

The sky is a little bluer,
Lessened our burden of care,
The world is made better today,
Because of somebody's prayer.

Our steps are a little lighter,
Our pathway grows more bright,
Because of somebody's prayer,
Life's wrong has changed to right.

The morning light is breaking,
After life's dark night,
Because of somebody's prayer,
We've scaled the mountain's height.

Someone is less lonely,
Someone's troubles are but few,
Because of somebody's prayer
We have hope again anew.

Because of somebody's prayer,
Perhaps, somebody's loved one,
Gave their heart and life to Jesus
And some lost soul was won!

The Loveliest Rose

Some storm clouds are needed,
Some rain in life, too,
Just to show us,
What God can do!
Some dark days are certain,
Some grief and some pain,
So God can make rainbows
After the rain.
Some trials and testings,
Some valleys below,
That raindrops may fall
And green grass may grow.
Afflictions are helpful,
Trust God who knows,
For thorns can display
The loveliest rose!

God is With Us

I'd hate to think I'd have to walk alone
Even for one minute,
For I know the sky Above
Has many storm clouds in it.
But, God said we're not alone,
And whatever we might face,
He gives the strength to stand,
And He gives "sufficient grace."
So we may be confident
That whatever lies ahead,
God leads us by the hand,
Just as He hath said.

Poetry

All the world's lovely things,
I shan't let pass by,
But, set their loveliness to pen,
Thereby to testify.
Rays of sunshine are fleeting,
Borne on whimsical, transient wings,
So 'tis a joy to place life's spirit
Into very permanent things!

Moments In Time

You ask me why I dillydally with verse and rhyme?
Some consider it a waste of time,
Oft it fails to earn one thin dime,
But, a better pastime one cannot find –

Sometimes ideas come on a whim,
Others at the drop of a hat,
Wherever I go, my writing goes, too,
And there's nothing better than that!

I like creating something that's mine,
Every now and then I write a quotable line,
The world to poets should be kind,
Because they catch "moments in time."

Spread Some Sunshine

Shed some light into the night,
Spread some love and cheer,
Make each day a little brighter,
And thus bring Heaven near!
Bear another's burdens,
Wipe away a tear,
Give hope unto the weary,
And chase away a fear!
Bring laughter to the lonely,
Comfort to ones who grieve,
And never-to-be-forgotten,
Will be the memories you leave.

Friends

I want to be a friend,
The kind that lasts from start to end,
The kind who stays when the going's rough,
The kind that's made of "sterner stuff."
The kind that keeps your best in mind,
The kind that encourages you strength to find,
The kind that helps you to see,
What your potential might really be,
The kind that helps you reach that star,
The kind who sends you high and far!

Before Television

Before television,
What did we do?
We watched the puppy
Play with a shoe.
We watched the kitten
Chase its tail,
We watched the cow
Kick the pail.
Hide and seek,
Water hose play,
That's how we passed
The time of day.
And when daylight faded,
With simple jars,
We caught fireflies –
Lanterns of stars.

Believe!

God doesn't expect our tears
When the sun doesn't shine,
Neither does He expect us to quit,
Nor waste away and pine.
But, God expects us to arise,
And with the faith of prayer,
To take a step believing
He can take us anywhere!

Roses in December

Friendships have I known
Whose lives have touched my own,
In such a very special way,
Adding brightness to each passing day,
Whose loving warmth and care
Helped make each day more fair.
Whose gentle loving hand
Uplifted and helped me stand,
Who walked with me that "extra mile"
And taught me still to smile –
Climbing mountains hand in hand,
And in valleys did by me stand,
And saw me safely through
Life's storms to a sky of blue,
So that my heart was warmed
Because of a friendship formed,
Leaving a sweetness to remember
As lovely roses in December.

Following Your Dream

Keep looking for life's rainbows,
Keep searching for that pot of gold,
Keep reaching for the stars
'Till the root of faith takes hold.
Though evasive seem the goals,
And illusive seem the dreams,
'Tis castles made of gossamer
That give to life its gleam.

Priceless Things

There are many gifts we may give,
And not spend one thin dime,
Like peace, hope, love and joy
Which take only of our time.
Those things that spring from within us,
Are those things so worth the while,
For friendship has no price tag,
And neither does a smile!
Anyone may give these gifts,
Be they a pauper or a king,
And the cost is nary a cent because,
Each is a priceless thing.

Who Put the Blue in the Sky?

Who put the blue in the sky,
Or makes a tiny sparrow fly,
Or hung the sun and moon and stars so high?
It has to be the Lord.

Who paints a pretty rainbow,
With colors of every hue,
And makes the flowers grow,
And springtime again renews?

Who holds the whole wide world,
In the hollow of His Hand,
And metes out the oceans,
And created each grain of sand.

Who clothes the lilies of the fields,
That toil not nor spin,
Yet, Solomon in all His Glory
Was not arrayed like one of them.

Who loved mankind so much,
He sent Jesus to die on a Cross,
So that we might be saved –
He paid sin's awful cost.

Who'll take the saved home
To Heaven's mansions in the sky?
It is our Lord and Savior,
He put the blue in the sky.

I Have Found the Way

You prayed for me today,
And light has shown my way,
New hope have I found,
New joy that knows no bound,
Because of loving care,
Because of answered prayer,
My night has changed to day,
And I have found the way!

That Special Someone

Every now and then, there is someone,
Who seems to be sent your way,
Just to add a touch of Heaven
To every passing day.
Who is so kind and loving
In all they say and do,
That times shared together
Become precious and too few.
You are just that special someone
Who makes the heart to sing,
Whose "special touch" leaves traces
Of love on everything!

Plant Flowers Where You Are

Wherever steps may lead in life,
Be it oe'r dry or stony ground –
Plant flowers wherever you are –
That faith may be found.

Just plant the seeds and watch them grow –
Make a home wherever you be –
And be it a cottage or a castle
'Twill be all the same to thee.

For happiness does not dwell without,
But, freely lives within –
And circumstances cannot daunt the soul –
That rests all trust in Him.

So make the desert a blooming rose,
Let its fragrance fill the air –
And whatever you touch along the way,
Will leave a garden of loving care.

Across the Miles

Although you are miles away,
In thought, I'm with you everyday,
I say a morning prayer for you,
That God may bless in all you do,
And when the evening sun sinks low,
I pray that you will always know,
That even though we are far apart,
You're always near within my heart.

A Friend is Many Things

A friend is many things,
But, most of all is there,
Ready to do whatever they can,
Just because they care.

A friend is a smile, a handclasp.
Reaching as a light in the night,
Midst a madly rushing world,
Is there to make things right.

A friend is like a rainbow,
A special promise from Above,
Another one of God's blessings –
Another glimpse of God's Love.

A Friend

When I was in need,
You were there.
When burdens pressed,
You said a prayer.
You stayed by my side
'Till my tears were dried,
And when I could not see,
You showed the path to me,
And you never once did stop
Until I reached the mountaintop.

The Forgiven Ones

Who are these?
From whence come they?
An innumerable host
In vast array.

Gathering in to Heaven,
At life's setting sun,
Passing through those pearly gates
They are the "forgiven ones."

Washed by the blood,
Saved by the Risen Lamb,
Justified by grace,
Heirs with the Great I Am.

"Of those given me," saith Jesus,
"I have lost none,"
Security of the believer,
They are the "forgiven ones."

Who are these?
From whence come they?
Those whose battles are won,
Lifted above life's fray.

Wearing starry crowns,
Clothed in robes of spotless white,
Now children of the day,
Who were once children of the night.

And if you do not know Him,
Just believe on God's only Son,
And dwell forever in Heaven someday,
As one of the "forgiven ones."

Two Eternities

We're traveling between two eternities –
We're either going to Heaven or Hell.
One path leads to destruction –
The other – the soul can say "all is well."

The narrow road leads to life everlasting,
It takes simple faith in God's Son,
But, the broad way leads downward,
Where fiery torments have only begun.

For the souls who have trusted in Jesus,
Heaven is their Destiny,
If you're standing in the Valley of Decision,
Which eternity will it be?

On one path, the roses bloom,
On the other, is the blackness of sin,
Now, we're traveling between two eternities,
One day, we'll never be able to choose again.

Get Heaven on the Line!

The signal's never busy,
Get Heaven on the line,
Talk to the Heavenly Father,
He'll answer every time.

Tell Him all your troubles,
And all that's on your mind,
Jesus will always listen,
No better friend can one find.

God will answer every prayer,
And send sweet peace sublime,
All your burdens will roll away,
And everything will turn out fine.

If we could talk to an important dignitary,
We'd be floating on cloud number nine,
But, we can talk to the Great Creator
Any day and anytime.

Heaven's telephone number is
Jeremiah 33 and 3,
"Call on Me and I will answer,"
So try it and you will see.

Behind all our fears and dread,
We'll find the clouds are silver lined,
The signal's never busy,
So get Heaven on the line!

God's "Love Letter" to Man

John 3:16 – so simple,
Even a child might understand,
Tells the way to everlasting life –
'Tis God's "love letter" to man.

It holds the promise
Of hope, peace, joy and light,
Of a Savior sent to earth,
To set the world aright.

In the covenant halls of Eternity,
The coming of Christ was planned,
As a Lamb slain from the world's foundation,
'Tis God's "love letter" to man.

Written with His precious blood,
Sealed by God's own Hand,
Agape Love – so high and great,
'Tis God's "love letter" to man.

That Day We Sing "Amazing Grace"

Often we get tired and troubled,
And weary in life's race,
But I'm looking unto a grander day,
When sin cannot efface.

When we'll be given a new name,
Known in Heaven's courts someday,
Where joy and love will overflow,
And perfect peace and rest will come to stay.

I'm looking unto a land,
Where the Saints and Angels trod,
I'm looking unto a City,
Known as the City of God.

Where our loved ones are now gathering,
Each one in their place,
I'm looking unto that day,
We sing "Amazing Grace."

It can't be too much longer,
I see victory up ahead,
Sin will all be vanquished,
And righteousness will reign instead.

The soul will be delighted
In that bright, eternal home,
Where there will be no need of the sun,
And life's darkness will be gone.

Where we'll join in happy chorus,
In sweet and rapturous song,
And tears will be wiped away,
As we join that ransomed throng.

We'll praise our dear Savior,
And we'll look upon His Face,
We'll be shouting "Glory, Hallelujah,"
As we sing "Amazing Grace."

No more aching, breaking hearts,
No more sorrows to be borne,
We'll just wake up in Heaven,
On some happy, golden morn.

Seems I can almost hear "Amazing Grace" echo
Throughout Eternity's Sacred Halls,
For when we sing "Amazing Grace,"
Everything will be worth it all.

The Crimson Cross

Jesus died at Calvary,
To save our souls so lost,
It seems I can almost see Him there
Upon that crimson cross.

Taking the guilt and shame of the world,
All alone in agony,
Shedding His blood that we might live
With Him for all Eternity.

Christ left the Glories of Heaven,
He paid sin's awful cost,
He became the Supreme Sacrifice,
Upon that crimson cross.

Friend, if you do not know Him,
If you're driven and tempest–tossed,
He went to Calvary for everyone
And died upon that crimson cross.

But, the story didn't stop there,
Else all would have been for loss,
Jesus arose from the grave,
And left behind the crimson cross.

There's no love like the love,
Of the man of Calvary,
And no grace like the grace
That is so rich and free.

How Come Somebody Like Him Loved Somebody Like Me?

How come somebody like Him,
Loved somebody like me?
'Tis the soul's great question
And Heaven's greatest mystery.

Jesus took a poor lowly beggar,
And made him a king,
He took a pauper,
And gave him everything.

He forgave my sins,
He nailed them to Calvary's tree,
And all I had to do
Was repent and believe.

He went to prepare a place for me,
Heaven's mansions, oh, so fine,
And, someday, all the splendors of Heaven
Will be mine.

How come somebody like Him,
Loved somebody like me?
For God so loved the world that He gave His Son,
To die at Calvary to set me free.

Why did Jesus leave Heaven,
Why did He love me so?
In all of Eternity
I don't guess I'll ever know.

Who Will Hold the Garlands?

Who will hold the garlands,
At the end of life's race?
Who will wear the crowning laurels,
For lives seasoned by God's grace?

Who will hold the garlands,
When we see Christ face to face?
Who will have lived to serve Him,
And have given Him first place?

Will we hear Christ say "Well done?"
Will we be crowned with the faithful and true?
What will be said about us,
When our lives are through?

In Gladiator times, the first to finish
Might not be the one to receive the prize,
But, the one who crossed with their torch still burning,
That's how it will be in God's eyes.

Not by works of righteousness which we have done,
For we are saved only by grace through faith,
But, let us reap a full reward,
Let us finish in first place.

Oh, who will hold the garlands,
In Heaven's bright, fair skies?
Who will be proclaimed the victors,
Who will win the prize?

The Darker It Grows, the Brighter He Shines

Jesus is a loving Savior,
Who helps in troubled times,
The darker it grows,
The brighter He shines.

There is peace in the valley,
And sweet rest for the soul,
Jesus is the Friend who stands by us,
Triumphant over the foe.

He keeps the love-light glowing,
Within this heart of mine,
He prepares a table for us,
And beckons "Come and dine."

He'll send out a rescue,
Every single time,
He will never leave us nor forsake us,
He is good and true and kind.

So when the world goes against us,
We can just say, "Never mind,"
Because the darker it grows,
The brighter He shines.

God's Never-Ending Story of Love

Jesus left His Throne in Heaven,
And all the splendors Above,
To die for our sins at Calvary,
It's the never-ending story of Love.

He'll take the saved home to Heaven,
To live in beautiful mansions Above,
To dwell eternally with Him—
It's the never-ending story of love.

For Christ came to save us,
From hell and all its doom,
He arose victoriously from the grave,
And He's coming back again soon.

He'll forgive our sins when we ask Him,
And give us life anew,
All because of His mercy and grace,
He will make all things new.

He sends His bountiful blessings,
And giveth peace, gentle like a dove,
It remains the greatest mystery—
God's never-ending story of Love.

The Eastern Sky

Jesus is coming again someday,
On this truth you can rely,
That's why I keep my eyes upon
The Eastern sky.

Saints and Angels will come with Him,
They shall descend from on High,
And take us home to Heaven,
To our mansions in the sky.

We shall behold Him,
The King in all His Glory,
And those who are saved,
Shall sing Redemption's Story.

The Shekinah light shall shine forth,
For lo, our redemption draweth nigh,
And we shall live forever,
In that sweet bye and bye.

Until then I'll wait and pray,
And watch the Eastern sky,
With hope fixed on that bright land,
Where our souls shall never die.

Jesus may come any morning, noon, or night,
He can be your Savior, too,
Give your heart to Him today,
So that He'll be coming for you.

Now's the Best Time to Kneel

When the road your traveling,
Seems to be all uphill,
That's the time to talk to Jesus,
That's the best time to kneel.

When troubles surround you,
Say to your soul, "Be still,"
As we wait upon God to answer,
For that's the best time to kneel.

No problem is too big for God,
No problem is too small,
Bring your burdens unto Jesus,
Who'll hear our every call.

So when we face life's giants,
And so inadequate we do feel,
That's when God's power is greatest,
And that's the best time to kneel.

Ask Jesus to be your Savior,
God's Love is so very real,
Today is the day of Salvation,
And now is the best time to kneel.

God's Sundry Names

He is the Lord of Lords,
And King of Kings,
He is the Great Creator,
And the Prince of Peace.

He's the Alpha and Omega,
And the Great I AM,
He's the Sacrificing Savior,
And the Risen Lamb.

He's the Everlasting Father,
The Good Shepherd is He,
Jehovah, Mighty God, the Messiah,
The Man of Calvary.

He's the God of our Fathers,
And the truest Friend,
His Name is Wonderful,
And His Kingdom hath no end.

He is the Lily of the Valley,
And sweet Sharon's Rose,
The bright Morning Star,
And the Victor over foes.

He was a Babe in the manger,
And the Crucified One,
King of the Jews, Yahweh, Elohim,
God's Only Begotten Son.

Continued

He's the Great Physician,
And the Mender of Broken Hearts,
Our Guide unto Death,
Jesus, the Christ, Who art.

He's the Fairest of Ten Thousands,
He is known as Faithful and True,
He is also our Judge,
Our Help in times of trouble, too!

And whosoever believeth in Him,
Shall have everlasting life,
His name is Immanuel,
He's the answer to life's strife.

He is our Refuge and Comforter,
And great Potentate is He,
Yet, He was also known as "Stranger,"
For He lived in obscurity.

He is the Way, the Truth and the Bread of Life,
The Holy One, our High Priest,
Our Advocate and Intercessor,
Whose Kingdom shall not cease.

And when we get to Heaven,
We shall see Him as He is,
The King in all His Glory,
Who would dare to miss all of this?

"

"Good-Night" Here, "Good Morning" There

Did you ever stop to think
About God's tender care,
For though we say "good-night" here,
We'll say "good-morning" there.

God holds all our tomorrows,
In his loving Hand,
For the saved, there is only goodness
In the pattern He has planned.

There are mansions awaiting,
And gates made of great pearls,
The streets are made of purest gold,
Oh, the beauty of God's new world.

So though here darkness comes,
And we must say good-bye,
In the morning we shall awaken
To Heaven's unclouded skies.

Continued

Trials will all be ended,
And sin will be no more,
Loved ones will be waiting for us,
On Heaven's golden shore.

There'll be no pain or sickness,
Nor death to knock on our mansion door,
And we shall live with Jesus
In joy forevermore.

So when they ring those golden bells,
Away my soul shall fly,
And God Himself shall wipe
The tears from my eyes.

You think that God doesn't know,
The sorrow that we bear,
Why, we only say "good-night" here,
To say "good morning" there.

God Specializes in Broken Things

When troubles overwhelm you,
And your heart has no song left to sing,
Bring your cares to Jesus,
He specializes in broken things.

He will heal your hurting heart,
And mend your broken wings,
He will make you fly again,
Trust in Him for everything.

Bring Him life's broken pieces,
Let Him put your life together,
He is the truest Friend,
Not just one that's fair-weather.

You may think you're too sinful,
And undeserving of God's grace,
But, not one of us is worthy,
Only Christ's blood can one's sins erase.

A broken and contrite heart,
God will not despise,
For each repenting sinner,
Is precious in His eyes.

Make God your Heavenly Father,
His children are dear to His heart,
His love, peace, joy, and grace,
To us He will impart.

No problem is too small or great,
For God can fix anything,
So place life's pieces in God's Hands,
For He specializes in broken things.

This Ol' World is Perishing

I have my Dad to thank for the idea of this poem.

This ol' world is perishing,
Someday, it will be no more,
This ol' world is perishing,
As sure as two and two make four.

Troubles on every hand,
All is subject to decay,
Rumblings of wars and devastation,
We hear of disasters every day.

But, someday, there'll be a new Heaven and earth,
One that shall not pass away,
God's love and joy and peace
Will finally come to stay.

This corruption shall put on incorruption,
And this mortal, immortality,
And we will say, "O death where is thy sting,
O grave, where is thy victory?"

And we shall be changed to be like Him,
In the twinkling of an eye,
God will come in great power and Glory,
From yonder in the skies.

Yes, this ol' world is perishing,
Someday, it will be no more,
This ol' world is perishing,
As sure as two and two make four.

Don't Miss Life's Song

We grow and live and learn,
Soon earth's fleeting time is gone,
We've only one life to live,
Don't miss life's song.

Take time to smell the roses,
Spread your wings and fly,
Make your dreams come true,
Hold to ideals that are high.

Hear the songbirds singing,
Feel the sunshine on your face,
And let your life be seasoned
With daily notes of grace.

And when troubles beset you,
And everything goes wrong,
Keep trusting in Jesus,
And wait for the breaking of dawn.

Makes Jesus your Savior,
And Heaven your eternal home,
But, whatever do you, remember,
Don't miss life's song!

Calvary Was All Uphill

When my cross grows heavy,
And obstacles hinder my way,
Lord, help me to remember that Calvary,
Was uphill all the way.

Christ was beaten by scourging,
But, was compelled to walk up Calvary's road,
He was too weak to bear His cross,
And fell beneath the load.

Nails pierced His Hands and Feet,
He was mocked and scorned,
In pain and agony, Jesus tossed—
He wore a crown of thorns.

The Lord never promised a flower-strewn pathway,
But, that He would see us through,
So help me remember Calvary,
When I need a friend so true.

And when storm clouds gather,
And the suns fails to cast a single ray,
Help me to remember that Calvary
Was uphill all the way.

For whatever trials I must face,
Or troubles that come my way,
They can't compare with Calvary,
And the price Christ had to pay.

So, Lord, oft remind me,
Of how Jesus loves me, still,
He went to the Cross to die for my sins,
Though Calvary was all uphill.

The Roll Call of the Faithful

We'd be proud to be in Who's Who's,
Or inducted into the Hall of Fame,
But, on the "Roll Call of the Faithful,"
Will God call your name?

Here we own houses and lands,
And seek after fortune and fame,
But, will our coffers be full in Heaven?
Are we willing to suffer loss for Heaven's gain?

Will you stand with Abraham, Isaac, and Jacob?
Crowned with the faithful and true,
Called a friend of God,
Can God depend on you?

If we're faithful over a few things,
God will make us ruler over many,
Let your light so shine
And your rewards will be more than plenty.

Many live their lives in obscurity,
Where few even know their name,
But, they'll be known in Heaven,
For just "a cup of water" given in Jesus' name.

On the "Roll Call of the Faithful,"
Will your name be found?
Remaining ever true and faithful,
Wearing a white robe and starry crown.

The Valley You Brought Me Through!

Lord, you've walked with me,
When friends were oh, so few,
You held my trembling hand,
You gave me Hope anew.

And Thy "grace was sufficient,"
Just like You've always said,
I trusted in Your Promises,
And "beside still waters" I was led.

You were my truest friend,
When no other Friend would do,
And with an outstretched Arm,
You led me safely through.

And though it was so wide and deep,
In that valley of despair,
My faith was sustained,
Just knowing that You were there.

And should I become a worldly success,
Or attain great fortune and fame,
I'll always remember the valley,
In which you dried my tears and eased my pain.

And no matter where life's pathway winds,
I'll always come back to view,
Just where it was You brought me from,
And the valley you brought me through.

Now my heart overflows with happiness,
Because the skies are oh, so blue,
But, Lord, I'll always remember
The valley You brought me through.

Are You Saved?

It is appointed unto man to die,
Be they a king or a knave,
But, where will you spend eternity?
Are you saved?

Is your soul safe in Jesus,
When roll Jordan's stormy waves,
Can you call Him your Lord and Savior?
Are you saved?

No question matters more,
No matter is quite so grave,
What will your answer be?
Are you saved?

John Harper, in 1912 was on board the *Titantic*,
When it sank, he was very brave,
Calling out to another who, too, was sinking
"Are you saved?"

The man twice answered, "No,"
Tossed about by tempestuous wave,
John Harper told him how to be "born again,"
And the man was saved.

The man was later rescued,
But, John Harper slipped to a watery grave,
But, the last words from this hero were
"Are you saved?"

No matter the good you do,
It's only by grace through faith,
That you'll pass through Heaven's gates,
Friend, are you saved?

The Greatest Love Story Ever Told

Jesus was born in a manger,
He was the Promised King,
Because God so loved the world,
Of Redemption I can now sing.

Jesus was crucified on a cruel cross,
By a world grown hard and cold,
Yet, He lay down His life for us,
'Tis the greatest Love Story ever told.

Salvation's gift is unspeakable,
Nor can any language express,
The depth and height of God's Love,
That saves us from Hell's abyss.

And, someday, because of God's grace,
I shall walk on Heaven's streets of gold,
And live with Christ forever and ever,
'Tis the greatest Love Story ever told.

Jesus left His Throne in Heaven for you,
Won't you ask Him to save your soul?
Agape Love—so high, so strong,
'Tis the greatest Love Story ever told.

That Hallelujah Choir

Someday, I'll sing like an angel,
With a voice that does not tire,
For one day you will find me,
Joining in Heaven's Hallelujah Choir.

I'll be safe at home with Jesus,
When this ol' world's on fire,
Singing the sweetest music ever heard,
In that Hallelujah Choir.

The redeemed will be gathered for all aye,
And what sweet communion shall transpire,
As we join in glad chorus
Of that Hallelujah Choir.

Jesus is His Name

He makes the flowers bloom,
He paints the rainbow after the rain,
He fills the air with sweet perfume,
Jesus is His Name.

He went to Calvary for you and me,
He took our sin and shame,
He suffered on a cruel Cross,
Jesus is His Name.

He pardons our transgressions,
He removes sin's stain,
He was victorious over Hell and the grave,
Jesus is His Name.

He hung the stars, sun, and moon so high,
He is always the same,
He'll take the saved to Heaven when we die,
Jesus is His Name.

He left Heaven's ivory palaces,
To come into this world of woe,
And He still hears a sinner's prayer,
Because He loves us so.

It remains the greatest mystery,
Why He left Heaven and came.
But, God so loved He gave His Son,
And Jesus is His Name.

Where No Ill Winds Blow

No ill winds in Glory,
No ill winds will blow,
No more pain nor sickness,
Like we oft know here below.

No more tears nor sorrows,
No troubled waters to overflow,
No ill winds in Glory, Lord,
No ill winds will blow.

No more trials or testings,
No more battles, no more foe,
No ill winds in Glory, Lord,
No ill winds will blow.

No more of sin and darkness,
No more valleys, so low,
No more rocky mountains steep,
No ill winds will blow.

No more tempestuous storms,
That war against the soul,
No disappointments nor discouragements,
No more of this world's woe.

No partings with wreaths of death,
No heartaches shall we know –
Where the roses will bloom forever,
And no ill winds will ever blow!

Still, Stilling the Storms

When I lean on Jesus,
My heart is made ever warm,
My troubles just melt away,
For God is still, stilling the storm.

Through trials and temptations,
He keeps me from danger and harm,
Walking daily by my side,
Safe from all alarm.

He says, "Peace be still,"
And the winds and waves obey,
"Be of good cheer, it is I,"
Are the words I hear Him say.

Of the believing souls,
He has not lost one,
All who've trusted in Him,
Shall see Him at life's setting sun.

Still holding my trembling hand,
Still wiping my weeping eye,
Still, stilling the storms of life,
Keeping me in the "eye."

Oh, that I might serve Him more,
For me, at Calvary He died,
Still, He's still, stilling the storms,
With His Love so deep and wide.

But Never Again!

They gambled for His garments,
But never again.
Pilate pronounced on Him a scourge,
But, never again.
They placed a Crown of Thorns upon His Brow,
But, never again.
Nails pierced His Hands and Feet,
But, never again.
They pierced His Side with a spear,
But, never again.
They gave Him vinegar for thirst,
But, never again.
He wore a mock purple robe,
But, never again.
For our sins, He was Crucified,
But, never again.
They sealed Him in a tomb,
But, never again.
In great clouds of Glory,
He will come again,
Repent and believe,
Because after His second coming,
He will never come again.
He will reign as King of Kings,
With royal Diadem –
Yes, they took His Robe away once,
But, never again!

I'll Be There!

I'll be there:
    when God makes up His jewels,
And they crown Him King of Kings,
When our joy is made complete
And the hosts of Heaven sing!

When the book of life is opened,
And I hear him call my name,
When all of Heaven cries,
"Worthy is the Lamb that was slain."

When the morning stars sing together,
And loud Hosannas ring,
And the ransomed souls with me
Unto Him I bring.

I'll be there when that White City,
In its Glory cometh down,
And I'll be there when
We exchange our ol' cross for a crown.

I'll be there when He wipes all tears away,
I'll be there when our loved ones
Are gathered together
For all aye.

I'll be there:
When Heaven's gates are opened wide,
And all the redeemed of all the ages
Step safely inside.

When Christ leads us through those mansions
And we sing a new glad song,
When life's night is vanquished,
And right triumphs over wrong.

And when we cast
    Our crowns at Jesus' Feet,
And be arrayed in robes of purest white,
I'll be there when His Righteousness
Breaks forth as morning light.

And I'll be there when the sky is parted,
Rolled back as a scroll,
And when my Lord comes again
To claim my ransomed soul!

He Speaks to Me

Sometimes God speaks in a still, small voice,
So that my aching heart doth rejoice,
Sometimes in a mighty rushing wind,
To show to me that He's my dearest Friend.

Sometimes in the lightning and thunderclaps,
Or in the lone seagulls cry,
When the storm clouds threaten,
Or clouds just pass idly by.

Sometimes in the eagle's flight,
Or in the sparrow's broken wing,
Sometimes in the silence,
Or when Heaven's joy-bells ring.

Sometimes in rapturous chords,
Sometimes in tones so sweet and low,
But, always my Shepherd's
Loving voice I know.

Sometimes in the sunshine,
Sometimes in the rain,
Sometimes in the peak of health,
Sometimes midst life's pain.

But, this I know, that when He speaks,
His Grace He doth impart,
For I know He speaks to me,
From a voice within His heart.

Carry On

When I feel discouraged,
With the joys of living gone,
Seems I hear my Heavenly Father say,
My child, just carry on.

Once I, too, grew weary,
When I walked up Calvary's road,
But, My grace is "all sufficient"
And I will carry your load.

And so I lift my daily Cross,
For by faith I can see,
That life's troubles are trite
Compared to God's Eternity.

When sorrows come,
And life's been robbed of song,
Seems I can hear Jesus say,
My child, just carry on.

Morning will soon be breaking,
Just over the Crystal Sea,
Night will soon vanish
Into Heaven's bright Eternity.

Carry on when your heart is breaking,
Carry on through the tears,
For God has promised to walk with us,
All down through the years.

Carry on through the trials,
And when things go so wrong,
Just weather the storm …
My child, just carry on.

God Rules Both Night and Day

Lord, when my soul is faint,
And I know not what to ask,
Grant me strength to overcome,
And grace to meet the task.
So weak and undone am I,
Yet, strong when You're by my side,
Thou art a mighty Refuge,
The Rock in which to hide.
Grant me wisdom to see Thy Light,
Resolve to walk Thy way,
Courage to face tomorrow, knowing,
You rule both night and day.

Keep Your Eyes Upon the Shore

When thunder claps the sky,
When waves are threatening nigh,
When the heart can bear no more,
Faith can see the shore!

Never give up 'till the battle be won,
Fight until the setting sun,
Never mind the storm's wild roar,
Just keep your eyes upon the shore!

For faith will dawn a brighter day,
Sweet victory will come your way –
And doubt will not linger anymore,
Where faith hath seen the shore!

Faith

When there is no light,
Faith can see.
When the valley is low –
Faith comforts me.

When eyes are dim,
When storms arise –
Faith is the strength
That clears the skies!

Faith is the victory
In trial or test –
For every doubt –
Faith answers YES!

If

If I can keep one heart from breaking,
If I can dry a tear,
If I can hold a trembling hand,
If I can calm a fear …

If I can shed some ray of hope,
Or bring joy into some heart,
If I can aid a weary soul,
If I can do a part …

To make life a little better,
And make skies not so gray,
To make this world a better place
Because I have lived today …

If I can shine a light in darkness,
If I can point the way,
If I can put a smile upon a face,
Or lead some lost soul that's gone astray …

If I can comfort some lonely heart,
And in petition, lift them up when I pray,
I will have cast bread upon the waters
That will return again, someday.

If I can lift up the fallen,
Or give "just a cup of water" in His Name,
If I can win some lost soul to Jesus,
Then I shall not have lived in vain!

He Understands and Cares

I saw my child's tear-filled eyes,
For some problem beyond his control,
Searching with such a hopeless gaze,
And great pity filled my soul.

The problem, small and simple,
His capacity could not bear,
But, overwhelmed his tiny frame,
So loaded down with care.

Then I thought of God, our Father,
Who sees the answers plain,
Whose tender love and mercy
Bid spare us needless pain.

Seeking to lift our yoke,
For His burden borne is light,
Reaching out to wipe the tear
That falls at darkest night.

If You Pass a Stranger

If you pass a stranger
Do not bid adieu,
But, make him feel welcome,
Someday, you may be a stranger, too.

If you pass one laden
With an extra heavy load,
Help him bear his burden,
You, too, may walk a weary road.

If you pass one lonely,
Be a kind, compassionate friend,
Make him feel needed,
And comfort swiftly send.

If you pass one in despair,
Say for him a prayer,
That he might lift eyes of faith,
And find solace there.

If you pass one in want,
Give from all you have in store,
For casting bread upon the waters
Will only bring you more!

Assurance

With every question to arise
In the mind of doubt,
Let the mind of faith be assured
That God has the answer.

Right is Right, and It Wrongs Nobody

Lovingly dedicated to my Grandmother Hixon

"Right is right, and it wrongs nobody,"
My Granny Hixon used to say,
You'll have to get up mighty early to beat that one,
Because right doesn't come in shades of gray.

Right is right, and it wrongs nobody,
These words are as "good as gold,"
Do right by your fellow man,
In the Good Book we are told.

Obey what the Blessed Lord tells you,
Stand for the good and true,
Be numbered with the faithful,
Be Christ-like in all you do.

Right is right, and it wrongs nobody,
'Tis food for thought to the soul,
God and you are a majority
In any crowd; that always know.

Right is right and it wrongs nobody,
You will meet your reward someday,
A Crown of Righteousness reserved against,
That Great Judgment Day.

Right is right and it wrongs nobody,
Like Daniel, dare to stand alone,
And keep up the good fight of faith,
Until the Lord deems fit to call you home.

The Good Left Behind

Judge not a life
By the length of stay,
But, by the good done
Along the way.
By the faith shown,
By the courage wrought,
By the deeds done,
By the good sought.
By the witness given,
By the souls won,
By the work for Jesus
That was done.
Years don't really matter,
Keep that in mind –
A lifetime is only …
The good left behind.

Making Diamonds

Diamonds are pressured stones,
In rival standing alone,
Esteemed for brilliance of light,
In spectrum's array shown.

Heat and pressure serve
But to perfect the gem,
As should trials and tests
Refract prism's light of Him.

Great force and fires are needful
Though they try the very soul,
For the substance making diamonds
Is akin to "simple coal."

The Keeper of the Storm

Though storms of life will blow,
Though my spirit is bowed low,
Still, I do not fear,
His Presence hovers near,
For I know the Keeper of the storm.

I'll trust Him all the way,
Through darkness unto day,
For lo, the clouds will break,
And reveal not one mistake,
For I know the Keeper of the storm.

Pearls of Great Price

A pearl had its rudiments
As a particle of rock or sand,
Introduced into the oyster shell
As an object of obstruction,
Until that thorn of affliction was transformed
Into the valued, rare and beautiful pearl.
Should not we, too, turn adversity to advantage,
Forbidding infirmity to hinder maturation,
So that in time, afflicted lives
Will yield pearls of great price?

Success

I'll not measure my success
By trophies that I've won;
Nor by a lengthy list,
Of the things that I have done.
I'll not reckon worth
By battle scars endured,
Nor medals awarded me
For evils that were cured.

But, I'll count my life successful,
If I consistently give my best,
And lean on Christ to be my strength
Through every trial and test.
I'll count my life successful,
To faithfully run life's race,
And to hold up high that Rugged Cross
As the emblem of "saving grace."

I've Never Been Lonely

As I travel on life's journey,
And I look back on the years,
Jesus has been with me
Through the smiles and through the tears.
In calm or stormy weather,
He has always seen me through,
And I've never been lonely,
With a Friend so true.
And when that last step is taken
Over Jordan deep and wide,
I know He'll be with me –
Forever by my side.
And, when someday I see Him,
This one thing I'll say –
Thank, you dear Jesus
For leading me all the way.
For never leaving nor forsaking,
For always remaining true,
And in every darkest night,
For making Thy Light shine through.
I know I can never repay You,
But, this one thing I'll do –
I'll love You more and more
Now and eternity through.

He is There

He is there, when storm clouds gather,
He is there, when friends are few,
He is there, when the heart is breaking,
He is there, to see us through.

He is there, when life's night is upon us,
He is there, our hope to renew,
He is there, when the dawn is breaking,
'Till the sky turns once again blue.

He is there, through trials and temptations,
He is there, our burdens to bear,
He is there, to give grace sufficient,
He is there, to answer every prayer.

He is there, when the road seems long,
He is there, to give us a song,
He wraps His loving Arms about us,
He is there, to right the wrong.

And He'll be there, when this life is over,
There, to stem Jordan's swelling tide,
In rapturous joy, the saved shall meet Him,
For He'll be there, waiting on life's "other side."

When We Can't, Heaven Can

When we're tired and weary, Lord,
And need Thy strength to stand,
When no power on earth can help us,
Heaven can.

When we need a Friend so true,
Someone to hold our trembling hand,
Someone to see our battles through,
Heaven can.

When we need grace for life's trials,
Light for the way,
Comfort midst sorrow,
God will show us the way.

His love will go where
Nothing else will dare,
It led Jesus to Calvary,
Your's and my sins to bear.

God can mend the brokenhearted,
And help to ease life's pain,
So when hope grows dim,
Just call out His sweet Name.

Help us see with eyes of faith,
The life that You have planned,
And to always remember, when we can't,
Heaven can.

No One Worthy But the Lamb

There was silence in Heaven,
No one worthy could be found,
To open the Great Book sealed with seven seals,
No one was worthy, but the Lamb.

Jesus is the Son of God,
Yet, He's also the Great I AM,
Lord and Savior and Great Creator,
And there's no one worthy but the Lamb.

Slain from the world's foundation,
Christ fulfilled God's Redemptive Plan,
He became the Supreme Sacrifice for our sins,
And no one is worthy, but the Lamb.

No one is worthy but the Lamb,
Praise be unto His Holy Name,
For no thing in Heaven, or earth or under the earth,
Is worthy, but the Lamb that was slain.

Oh, How He Loves the Little Lambs

I know that Jesus loves me,
For the Bible tells me so,
His Love led Him to Calvary,
To save my sin-sick soul.

I know God cares for the sparrow,
And feeds it by His Hand,
He clothes the lilies of the field,
Which neither toil nor spin.

God loves all the sheep of His pasture,
But, nearest and dearest to the heart of God,
Are the little Lambs, (children) whose Angels,
Always behold the "Face of God."

More Than Enough

Never does God ask
Above what we can do,
Never does He require
Without "grace" to see us through.
Never does a task bid us
Bear too great a cross,
Never is labor for Him
Wrought in vain for loss.
Never does a trial
Exceed what we can bear,
Never does the pathway lead
Beyond His loving care.
Never must we tread
Life's staircase all alone,
Never will His footsteps cease
To lead us safely home.

Time is Not

Man measures space and calls it time,
We speak of the length of this or that,
But, God above who surveys the scene,
Sees those arbitrary lines as but markers,
To be lifted at life's closing day,
For with God … time is not.

A Love So Great

A love so great …
That Jesus endured the pain and agony of Calvary's Cross,
And although legions of Angels would have come to His rescue,
He didn't call for them.

A love so great …
It makes even the vilest sinner clean,
who comes trusting in Him through repentance and faith.

A love so great …
It reached to the dying thief of the cross,
who was saved, and met Jesus that day in Paradise.

A love so great …
God's only begotten Son was rent from God's own heart.

A love so great …
That neither height, nor depth, life or death,
principality nor power can ever separate us
from the love of God which is in Christ Jesus.

A love so great …
It saves every lost sinner who comes to Him.

A love so great …
it will go on and on and on and never end.

No Time

There is no time for doubting,
No time for tarried step,
No time for sloth or slumber,
For souls must needs be kept.
There is no time for fainting,
No time for finished work,
Until God says all is done –
Duty we must not shirk.
No time for discouragement,
No time for weary sighs,
No time for any "letting up,"
Until Jesus breaks the skies.
So keep on working brother,
Steadfastly take your stand,
Ever ready as Joshua and Caleb,
To claim the Promised Land.

Compassion

It's easy to speak of faith
When not facing any test,
Or boast of strength and fortitude,
When with great ease we rest.
It's easy to fear not darkness
When brightly shines noonday,
And easy to speak of trust
When no storms have crossed our way.
It's easy to remain untroubled,
When no knock is at our door,
And easy to bear our crosses,
When blessings around us pour.
It's easy to view the valleys
From the mountain's lofty peak,
And easy to find the way,
When there is no need to seek.
Wait not 'till lightning strikes
To drive home the lesson clear –
With compassion reach out now
To someone standing near!

My Brother's Keeper

For all whose paths I cross each day,
With befitting words, let me convey,
An understanding to meet each need,
Coupling comforting thought with noble deed.
Expending self in service to others,
Seeking to uplift my lonely brothers,
To fill a void, lighten a load,
To help ease care along life's road.
If another's gain be my expense,
No matter, rewards will follow hence.
So I'll scatter my jewels, bestow every good,
And be all that my brother's keeper should.

I Will Call You Friend

When I think of Your infinite wonders, Lord,
To my mind, it is so deep,
So I find I must simply trust
In Your "sufficient grace," to ever keep.
Your Love covers humanity,
Yet, I know Your single touch,
You died for all, this I know,
But, for one, just as much.
I view Your wondrous works,
All of creation by Your Power –
Yet, that same Hand fashioned
The delicacy of a flower.
I see Your might displayed
Over a Universe vast and wide –
And yet, I feel Your tender love –
As the Refuge in which I hide.
For most of all, I know You, Lord,
In a very simple and personal way –
My God and my Redeemer,
Yet, my Companion day by day.
And I am sure when I see You,
When I come to this journey's end –
Though King of Kings and Lord of Lords –
I will also call you "Friend."

The Royal Family

Are you a member of the Royal family?
Do you bear a likeness to the King?
Do you belong to the family of God?
Does your life, glory unto Him bring?

Are you recognized in the courts of Heaven?
Does everyone there know your name?
Are you a joint-heir with Christ?
Someday with Him to reign.

Is your name written down
In the Lamb's Book of Life?
Have you been saved by Jesus' blood?
Do you have eternal life?

Does your daily conversation,
Reflect the Father up Above?
Do the things you say and do,
Tell about Calvary's Love?

Do you do what Jesus would do?
Do you seek the Father's Will?
Do you follow in Jesus' steps?
Are you His ambassador of goodwill?

Does He call us brother, sister,
Mother, friend –
Because we seek to walk with God,
Unto our journey's end?

Are we a member of the Royal Family?
Do we bear a likeness to the King?
Do you belong to the family of God?
Are you a child of the King?

At the Crossroads

Are you standing at a crossroads?
What choice will it be?
God is at the crossroads
Pointing toward Heaven's Eternity.

The devil's also at the crossroads,
Don't let satan gain the victory,
Don't reject God's only begotten Son,
But, choose upon Christ to believe.

As you stand and ponder,
Determining what will be your fate,
There's not a moment to be wasted,
Tomorrow may be too late.

Heaven's Angels are watching,
Those pearly gates are opened wide,
You've a Heaven to gain and a Hell to shun,
But, only you can decide.

Is your account all settled?
It was paid for long ago,
When Jesus died at Calvary,
To save your sin-sick soul.

The choice is yours; don't tarry,
For unbelief is the only reason why,
You'll miss all the joys of Heaven,
And that home up in the sky.

Despise Not the Day of Small Things

(Zachariah 4:10)

Despise not the day of small things,
As prayers of simple faith,
By them, great things are wrought,
By these single "notes of grace."
.

A diamond is made from a lump of coal,
A pearl, by a grain of sand.
Do not despise the day of small things,
Fashioned by God's loving Hand.

Despise not the day of small things,
By them, kingdoms rise or fall,
Simple acts of kindness,
Are recorded in Eternity's sacred Halls.

A great oak grows from an acorn,
A mighty tree from a mustard seed,
So begin today in some small way,
Then trust God for where it will lead.

Along Comes Jesus

Sometimes, when I'm discouraged,
And the sky turns oh, so gray,
Along will come Jesus
To chase the clouds away.

And when troubles come,
Often so hard to bear,
Jesus gives me strength to carry on,
And takes away my care.

And when the lightning claps,
And the thunder rolls,
Along will come Jesus
And His sweet peace I know.

And when my cross grows heavy,
And my heart is filled with fear,
Along will come Jesus,
To wipe away my tears.

For back when I was lost in sin,
Jesus showed me the way,
And I never will forget
That moment He heard this lost sinner pray.

And when I cross over Jordan,
I know I won't be alone,
Along will come Jesus
To carry me safely home.

And He Called It Calvary

Jesus came to die,
Upon a cruel tree,
God sent to us His love
And called it Calvary.

Why the Son of God should die
For a wretch like you and me,
That was God's gift of grace,
And love's great mystery.

'Twas just a simple cross,
Upon a lonely hill,
But, Jesus changed men's lives
And changes them still.

No merits can we plead,
Nothing deserving have we done,
To be visited by God Above,
By the gift of His only Son.

By the shed blood of Jesus,
Our sins are washed white as snow,
'Tis God's unspeakable gift
To us mortals here below.

Yes, God sent Heaven's jewel,
He deemed it best you see,
He sent to us His Love
And called it Calvary.

He Knows Just What To Do

When you are discouraged,
And helping friends are few,
Take your cares to Jesus,
He knows just what to do.

As a child brings his hurts,
For Mother to kiss away,
We have a Heavenly Father,
Who'll lift us above life's fray.

He will never leave nor forsake,
He is faithful and true,
He'll wipe the tears away
For He knows just what to do.

So when you walk through valleys,
God will see you through,
The sun will shine once again,
And the sky will turn to blue.

So if you are troubled,
And to life's answers you haven't a clue,
Just tell it all to Jesus,
He knows just what to do.

And when burdens press,
And the foes compass,
There is peace and joy in Jesus,
The kind that shall forever last.

Give Jesus all life's pieces,
He'll remake your life anew,
Let Him mend your broken heart,
For He knows just what to do.

Living Water

Jesus met a woman at the well,
He told her of living water that could set her free,
From the chains of sin that bound her,
If she would repent and believe.

Jesus said that water from the well,
Would makes one thirsty again,
But, living water that He offered,
Would be a fountain springing from within.

The woman said, "Come see a man
Who told all things that ever I did,
Is this not the Christ?"
The One Who was to come to die in our stead.

The woman at the well was saved that day,
But, well water could not save her poor lost soul,
For by grace are ye saved through faith,
For Christ is the fountain of the soul.

Living water, living water,
Living water for the thirsty soul,
Oh, the grace that saves us,
And Christ's touch that makes us whole!

My Soul Doth Testify

Thou art the Great Creator,
Who ruleth from on High,
Marvelous is Thy Handiwork,
The sun, moon, stars, earth and sky.

The hairs of our head are numbered,
Thou knoweth the way that I take,
Thou knoweth my downsitting and uprising,
And will never leave nor forsake.

Thy Name is Wonderful, Counselor,
Everlasting Father, and Prince of Peace,
Thy government shall have no end,
It shall only prosper and increase.

Thou calleth the stars by name,
And knoweth the heart that is tried,
Thou art from Everlasting to Everlasting,
And my soul doth testify.

Thy grace wrought so great a Salvation,
Not of works that we can claim,
Yet, Thou art not ashamed to call us brethren,
Or a people called by Thy name.

In life and in death, we praise Thee,
Who at Calvary for us died,
And someday, we shall go to Heaven,
Where our souls shall testify!

Songs in the Night

Blessed be the name of Jesus
Who giveth songs in the night,
For when things look bleakest,
He shines His guiding light.

Oh, how I love Jesus,
His power and greatness I proclaim,
He still saves every lost sinner,
Who calls upon his name.

He gives the strength to live by,
And the grace to die,
And will take my soul home to Heaven,
When I die.

So when life's troubles beset,
I lift my eyes unto Him,
His Glory never fades,
And His Truth shall never dim.

God watches over the sparrow,
And I know He cares for me,
Blessed be the name of Jesus
The Savior of Calvary.

He is a tender loving Shepherd,
Who makes the pathway bright,
He whispers sweet peace
And giveth songs in the night.

Can You Show Me The Way?

Can you show me the way to Calvary,
By the life that you live, by the good that you do,
By the words that you say,
By a faith that is true?

If I were to step into your shoes today,
Would they lead to Calvary?
For I am lost on life's road,
Can you point the way?

Can you show by example,
God's grace proffered me?
If I were to ask directions,
Would they lead me to Calvary?

I'm kind of in a hurry,
So I would like to know,
Which leads to Heaven,
Which way should I go?

Do I tend to the straight and narrow,
Or is the broad road right?
Which way leads to darkness –
Which way leads to light?

I stand in need of a friend,
Will you undertake the task?
Will Salvation fill the void in my life?
Is it something that will last?

Can you lead me to the One,
Who can take my sins away?
Don't wait 'till I decide on
A more convenient day.

Wait for the Morning

When you are tired and discouraged,
And it seems hope is almost gone,
Just wait for the morning,
And the breaking of the dawn.

God will give you grace for life's trials,
And the strength to carry on,
He will never fail nor forsake you,
He will right the wrong.

Someday, in Heaven, you will understand,
Just why the night was long,
So when life's troubles beset you,
Just keep on holding on.

Be strong and of good courage,
And God will give your heart a song,
If you just wait for the morning,
And the breaking of the dawn.

The Song of the Redeemed

I sing the song of my Redemption,
Of God's wondrous grace to me,
How Christ died to grant my pardon,
How He forgave my sins, and set me free.

It is the sweetest old, old story,
That tells through Christ is the victory,
Of how He forsook the splendors of Heaven,
To lay down His life for you and for me.

Let the bells of Heaven start peeling,
Let loud Hosannas ring,
For I sing the song of my Redemption,
That even the Holy Angels cannot sing.

It is a song of love unspeakable,
About the Lord of Lords and King of Kings,
And, someday, when my soul takes flight,
I'll be singing the song that the Angels cannot sing.

They can only look on at the grace He proffered,
They can only observe dark Calvary,
Things they have a desire to "look into,"
But, 'tis only the song of the Redeemed.

He Chose "a Cross"

He didn't choose greatness,
For to a lowly manger He came,
He didn't seek His own,
Nor did He choose fortune or fame.

But, He became obedient unto death,
For He had come unto "that hour,"
He didn't choose a flower-strewn pathway,
In which to demonstrate His Heavenly Power.

And in lonely Gethsemane,
When He sweat great drops of blood,
In agony His soul was tossed,
While He only sought our good.

"He was wounded for our transgressions,
And bruised for our iniquities,"
He lay down His life
To set our lost souls free!

And what He chose to show
Unto a world so lost –
The emblem of God's undying Love –
Was "a Cross."

Yes, at Calvary He chose
To bear sin's awful cost,
For the emblem of God's undying Love,
Was "a Cross."

Thirty Pieces of Silver

Judas sold our Savior,
For thirty pieces of silver,
With the promise to the Romans
Unto them, Jesus He would deliver.

The Son of God
Was betrayed by Judas' kiss,
Because of unbelief,
Judas chose Hell's great abyss.

For thirty pieces of silver,
There the story's told,
Judas rejected the Christ
Whose touch could have made him whole.

For thirty pieces of silver,
The deed was over and done,
Betrayed by the love of money,
Was God's only begotten Son.

Whatever stands in your way of belief,
Be it silver or gold,
That is the price you place
On the value of your soul.

In the Judgment Day, then
Where will be your coffers of gold?
Then, oh, what you'd give
In exchange for your soul!

Christ's Disciple Named Peter

Before one criticizes Peter,
Make this mental note,
At least he had enough faith
To get out of the boat,

And to go to Jesus,
Walking on the Sea of Galilee,
When he saw the waves so boisterous,
He feared, like you and me.

Everyone says St. Peter tends the pearly gates,
And this might not be such a hyperbole,
I'd be honored if Peter
Was one of the first that I should see.

And although Peter denied Jesus,
God later used him in a mighty way,
For when he preached at Penecost,
Three thousand souls were added unto the church that day.

God can take our failures,
And turn them inside out,
And shine His loving rainbow,
Far beyond the clouds of doubt.

And Jesus can still use us, too,
Though we be weary and battle worn,
For in the furnace of affliction,
Often great souls are born.

He Gave His Best For Me

Jesus went to Calvary,
From my sins to set me free,
I want to give my best for Jesus,
He gave His best for me.

For by grace through faith,
In Heaven, we shall someday be,
Not of works lest we should boast,
But, because of God's love for you and me.

God gave His only begotten Son—
And Jesus stepped down from His Heavenly Throne,
To come into a world of woe,
Our sins to atone.

So when I face life's giants,
I just remember Gethsemane,
Where Jesus sweat drops of blood,
And then went to Calvary.

I want to give my best for Jesus,
Who gave His best for me,
And so I'll lift my cross and follow Him,
Until His blessed Face I see.

Morning Will Come

When the night is long,
When hope seems to be gone,
Don't be discouraged,
Try to just carry on.

Troubles will soon pass away,
Our battles will be won,
Keep praying and trusting in God,
Morning will come.

The dawn will soon be breaking,
And life will be good again,
Sufficient grace God will give,
And help He will send.

The storms will pass over,
Out will come the sun,
And there'll be smiles instead of tears,
When morning shall come.

He Will Paint a Rainbow

God is our dearest Friend,
He cares like none other can do,
Trust Him on life's pathways,
And let Him paint "a rainbow" for you.

He knows our disappointments,
He knows our grief and pain,
He knows our trials and tests,
And giveth grace to sustain.

And He knows our sorrows,
And sees when each teardrop falls,
And, yet, He paints a rainbow
Through it all.

Yes, through it all,
We see God's Love shining through,
Trust Him through life's storms,
And He'll paint a rainbow "for you."

God's Thoughts Toward Us

(Psalm 139:17-18)

God's thoughts toward us
Are more than the sands of the sea,
Whether we sleep or wake,
Lord, we are still with thee.

In valleys so low,
Or on mountain's high,
God's Spirit hovers near,
His presence is always nigh.

So when you're feeling lonely and blue,
Remember the Friend who'll stand by you,
Who is faithful and true,
And will take good care of you.

God watches over the tiny sparrow,
How much more He cares for you and me,
God loved us so much He gave His Son,
To die for our sins at Calvary.

I'm Richer Than a King

I may be short on money,
But, I'm richer than a King,
I have the love of Jesus,
And I have everything.

My clothes may be threadbare,
But, of God's saving grace I sing,
I'm a child of the Heavenly Father,
Which makes me richer than a King.

I've got a mansion in Heaven awaiting,
A righteous robe and starry crown,
And nothing in this world can compare
To this joy I've found.

So looks can be deceiving,
For, someday, I'll walk on streets of gold,
And it will be worth all the heartaches
And troubles here below.

And so I count my many blessings,
For I'm richer than a King,
I have the love of family and friends,
And I have everything!

He Makes the Robin to Sing

He made the mountains and the trees,
He created summer, fall, winter and spring,
He owns the cattle on a thousand hills,
And He makes the robin to sing.

He is from everlasting to everlasting,
He has no beginning or end,
He is our Hope of Heaven Above,
And on earth, our dearest Friend.

The morning stars sing together,
The rocks of the fields, clap their hands,
As God's great Handiwork is displayed,
In sky and sea and land.

God watches over us night and day,
For we are sheltered under His Wing,
He sees a tiny sparrow's fall,
And He makes the robin to sing.

Time's Demise

I realized I am getting old,
When I didn't scoop up a tiny frog today,
Or blow the cotton puff off the stem,
Yelling at the baseball games has lost its allure,
As has eating "cotton candy" at the fair!
I decided not to walk the dog, as the sun was too hot,
Or run to the house from our roadside mailbox,
Or walk in the rain last rain shower.
I can no longer skate across the frozen lake,
Nor do I ride in a sled through the snow,
But, this one thing I've noticed,
Despite all these fading things,
Life grows sweeter as I go,
For I oft reminisce on scenes of childhood,
And sweet memories link past with present,
For as I'm nearing Heaven's eternal home,
I've found "the joys that last."

Grant Us...

Help in the time of trouble,
Peace midst the storm,
Victory in the day of battle,
Hope in despair,
Light in darkness,
Wisdom to apply knowledge,
Compassion on our needy brother,
Ways that acknowledge Thy paths,
A vision for the lost.
Fervent prayers that ask aright.
Strength to meet the tasks,
Mercy – Thy unmerited favor.
And grace that You might keep us
In the "Eye of the Storm."

You must be saved to reap the benefits of all these things. (John 3:16)

Lest I Forget

Make me a vessel for good,
Oh, Lord, I pray.
Give me Thy grace "sufficient,"
To meet the needs of everyday.
Casting all burdens upon You,
For Your burden borne is light.
Your Promises, remain, like the rainbow,
Equity, and Judgment and Right.
"Put my tears in a bottle." (Scripture)
Strengthen me to steadfast faith,
And, "Teach me to number my years," (Scripture)
Lest I forget.

When We Meet Again

When we meet again,
Our tears will be all wiped away,
Trials will all be over,
And there'll be peace at the end of life's way.

No ill winds will be blowing,
And troubles shall be no more,
That will be a happy reunion
As we gather on Heaven's fair shore.

The darkness of night will be over,
All work ceased and done,
No more heartaches or disappointments,
And a new life will be begun.

We'll meet again, God hath promised,
And time shall be no more,
And we shall love each other
Even better than before.

Oh, that day of rest and gladness,
Of perfect peace and joy and love,
We'll bask in the light of God's goodness,
In our blessed home above.

We'll lay life's crosses down,
At the blessed Savior's Feet,
We shall sing and we shall rejoice,
And our life will be made complete.

Sin will no more have dominion,
O'er those who have been saved by God's grace,
For them, there's a bright tomorrow,
And thank God, another "meeting place."

Good-bye For Now

Good-bye for now,
That's all I will say,
Until we meet again,
In Heaven's fair day.

Where we shall join hands again,
And nevermore say good-bye,
In that glad reunion day,
Up yonder in the sky.

Good-bye for now,
But this is not the end,
But, only the beginning
Of God's new world without an end.

Where there'll be no more tears,
Or sorrows to be borne,
The saved will just wake up in Heaven,
Some "happy morn."

The Four Of Us Know

We've all heard say that those in Heaven,
Would not come back if they could,
But, the four of us know of one –
Our Mother, who would.

If and when the kids were small,
And needed lots of care,
She'd have forsaken those streets of gold,
And those mansions all so fair.

Though the golden shores would have beckoned,
Where the artesian waters flowed,
She would have said, "Not now, Lord,
I must not, cannot go."

Another time, another day,
For I am needed most at home,
I know I must not stay,
For I cannot leave them all alone.

Continued

Little hearts and hands are depending,
On me to take life's hurt away,
I must go and paint skies of blue,
And chase away clouds of gray.

She would have missed the angels singing,
And talking with the Saints of old,
To come back into a life of care and trouble,
For the little ones, you know.

She would have seen all the splendors of Heaven,
And taken only a moment to decide,
And crossed back over Jordan,
With its valley deep and wide.

For when Heaven's gates were opened,
She would have chosen not to step inside,
As much as her soul longed for Heaven and home,
Her love would have spanned the Great Divide.

How She is Known

To some she was mother,
Daughter, sister, or wife,
But to those in her family,
She was their life.

Some say she was an angel,
Sent from Above,
But, to me she was "Mother,"
And the name meant love.

To some she was advisor and counselor,
Someone on whom you could depend,
But to those whom she loved,
She was known as "best friend."

With all of these names,
Oh, the pictures they paint,
But, in Heaven she's known,
As God's … blessed Saint.

Dedicated in loving memory of my Mother, Maxine Spryes Hixon —
the dearest and the best.

Heaven's Sweetest Rose

The sweetest rose on earth,
Was taken away,
Transplanted to bloom,
In Heaven's fair day.

Though hearts shall always miss her,
Still, we must say,
She now dwells in the presence of Jesus,
In that fair, unending day.

She bloomed in earth's sunshine,
But, now in God's light,
She thrives now in Paradise,
Untouched by sin's blight.

Gathered by the Holy Angels,
Carried to her home up Above,
She basks in God's goodness,
And is sheltered by His Love.

Nevermore to fear,
Harm or decay,
Moth or rust cannot corrupt
The treasures reserved in Heaven's bright day.

Eternally to bloom,
And never to fade away,
Transported to Heaven's Glory,
From a house made of just clay.

Raised in God's likeness,
Magnified by His power,
Clothed in His righteousness,
'Twas earth's sweetest flower.

My Mother was the sweetest rose on earth,
And when God chose to take her away,
He picked the dearest and loveliest of all,
To add to Heaven's bouquet.

An Old-fashioned Mother

I had an old-fashioned Mother,
Filled with beauty and grace,
With an old-fashioned "way of dress,"
How I loved her dear face.

With worldly things,
She was so "out of place,"
Yet, she witnessed to lost souls,
Of God's saving grace.

My old-fashioned Mother,
Was a gift from God Above,
For she wrapped us all,
In her old-fashioned love.

Her children all arise,
"How blessed" they say,
To have an old-fashioned Mother
Who so fervently prayed.

Thank God for my Mother
With her old-fashioned ways,
Who lived by the Bible,
All of her days.

I think in God's Heaven,
There'll be a special place,
For such a God-fearing Mother,
Filled with "uncommon faith."

When the Lilacs are in Bloom

How Mother loved the lilacs,
That smell of sweet perfume,
She talked about them oft,
When the lilacs were in bloom.

Pink and white flower clusters,
Made by God's own Hand,
Glistening in the morning dew,
Like pearls upon the sand.

In paradise, do you suppose,
The lilacs will be in bloom?
Making up a sweet bouquet,
In Heaven to find room.

They have a timeless beauty,
That does not fade away,
Like flowers here on earth,
That are subject to decay.

I'll meet Mother inside Heaven's Gate,
Where there will be no more gloom,
And we'll sit and talked as in days of yore,
And watch the lilacs bloom.

Looking Unto Jesus

If stars were always shining,
Or the sky was always blue,
I fear we'd fail to realize
Our "need" as we go through.
If all were smiles and laughter,
And never was shed a tear,
Our thoughts might be adrift
From Heaven's sights so dear.
If flowers always lined the way –
Paths trod without a thorn,
The bouquet we might gather
Might not our lives adorn.
For raindrops serve to reflect
That Heavenly home Above,
And imperfections only mirror
His pure and perfect Love.

Springtime in My Heart

In loving memory of my beloved son, Paul Maxwell Rhea,
(March 28, 1978 to October 7, 2000.)

On earth we had to say good-bye,
It's so sad we had to part,
But, because of you, there'll always be …
Springtime in my heart.

You were the sunshine of my life,
And I thought you hung the moon,
I glimpse our love in God's deep blue sky,
And in each flower that is in bloom.

"'Tis better to have loved and lost,
Than never to have loved at all,"
These words were penned by one who knew,
That love is worth it all.

Continued

And we shall meet again,
In that land so bright and fair,
Where we'll forget the tears we shed,
And the sorrows we had to bear.

You were my darling angel,
A gift from God Above,
Lent to me for a space in time,
For me to care for and love.

People ask me sometimes,
Just how I'm getting along,
But, you've left me with so many memories,
And life's loveliest of songs.

For though we had to say good-bye,
In my life you'll always remain a part,
For even death cannot eclipse,
The springtime in my heart.

'Till Things of Earth Shall Pass Away

For the saved:

Only a few more heartaches 'till Glory,
Only a new more teardrops 'till Heaven's bright day,
Only a few more trials and testings,
'Till things of earth shall pass away.

Only a few more valleys to walk through,
Only a few more miles to go,
No good-byes will there be spoken,
And no troubled waters shall overflow.

Only a few more storm clouds to gather,
'Till dark night turns into day,
Only a few more days of tribulation,
'Till things of earth shall pass away.

Only a Few More Miles To Go

Only a few more days of trouble,
Only a few more miles to go,
'Till I see Jesus who died to save me,
Only a few more ill winds to blow.

Only a few more hours of darkness,
Only a few more of life's woes,
Only a few more trials to face,
Only a few more heartaches below.

Only a few more sad disappointments,
Only a few more teardrops to fall,
Only a moment, 'till comes the morning,
Only a few more sorrows to befall.

Only a few more storm clouds to gather,
'Till I walk on streets of gold,
Just a few more sunsets behind the mountain,
With only a few more miles to go.

Carry Me ...
Until I Can Walk Again

Lord, when I grow weak,
And stumble along the way,
Give me "sufficient grace,"
Be Thou my Guide and Stay.

For in all Heaven and earth,
There is no dearer Friend,
And so I trust You to carry me,
Until I can walk again.

I don't deserve Thy Love and Grace,
Yet, Thy blessings you bestow,
You know where I've been,
And where e're my footsteps go.

Thou who watches over the sparrow,
Let Thy mercy upon me descend,
For I trust you to carry me,
Until I can walk again.

Isn't It Wonderful?

Isn't it wonderful
That good-byes aren't forever,
That we will join hands again,
In that sweet forever?

Isn't it wonderful Jesus came,
And took upon Himself our load of sin,
That He died to be the Victor,
That's He's coming once again?

Isn't it wonderful Heaven awaits,
With all its joys untold,
That we will sing that sweet story
With all the Saints of old?

Oh, won't it be wonderful there?
With never a burden or care,
Never a sorrow, never a tear,
Never a doubt, never a fear.

For Jesus, the Light,
Will shine on forever,
And the saved will rest
Beside that shining River.

For mansions await us,
God's Love will enfold us,
And we will join in
That Hallelujah chorus!

Through Jesus' Eyes

Let me see the world
Through Jesus' eyes,
Let me feel the great need,
And attend unto the cries.

Let me be His Hands and Feet,
An ambassador of Goodwill,
And tell the lost of Jesus,
How their lives His Love can fill.

Let me see the world
Through Jesus' eyes,
And have compassion for humanity,
For whom at Calvary He died.

Let me reach out to my brother,
Let me be of Christ's mind,
'Till His Love shall compass the whole
Of all mankind.

Peace with God

Have you made peace with God?
That's the great question of the soul –
Will you be safe in the Arms of Jesus
While the eternal ages roll?

Have you accepted Christ as your Savior?
Have you been cleansed by His blood?
Have you knelt at the cross of Calvary,
And been washed by that crimson flood?

Have you made peace with God?
Nothing matters more, you know,
Is thy heart right before God?
Have your sins been made white like snow?

Everywhere There is Love

You watch over the tiny sparrow,
You clothe the lilies, so fair,
Everything is affected by Thy Touch,
And we Thy Image bear.

You send so many blessings,
So many, in a single day,
The earth is filled with Thy Goodness,
Thy Handiwork is on display.

You hung the sun, moon and stars so high,
And made a Heaven for us Above,
For, oh Lord, I catch a glimpse of Thee
Everywhere there is love.

Almost

Almost never won a battle,
Never tasted victory sweet,
Never attained the mark,
Never reached time's peak.

Almost is filled with regrets,
Of opportunities passed on by,
And the only fruit "almost" bears,
Are tears and endless sighs.

Almost is a word "at risk."
For costly be life's run,
To find "almost" a synonym
For empty and undone.

Almost had a view of Heaven,
But, chose not to step inside,
Almost is but unbelief,
And must "without" abide.

Living on the Other Side

I was filled with doubts and confusion,
It seemed, there was no place to hide,
But, then I met Jesus at Calvary,
And I am living on the other side.

All my time had been spent
On life's highways so wide,
But, now I have a golden tomorrow,
For I live on the other side.

Old ways and old paths I've forsaken,
For Jesus, for my sins hath died,
I've given Him life's broken pieces,
And now live on the other side.

On the other side of Calvary,
I know His love so deep and wide,
And I sing of the grace that saved me,
For I'm living on the other side.

Crosses, Then Crowns

When I'm low in spirit,
And this ol' world gets me down,
I always remind myself,
First the crosses then the crowns.

So through every trial and test,
May I come forth like gold,
My hope set on that fair land,
That is the sweet home of my soul.

May I lift my cross and follow Him,
Wherever His footsteps lead,
To be counted as faithful and true,
Is all that I'll ever need.

The servant is not above his Master,
They treated Christ shamefully, you know,
So whatever hardships I must endure,
I just remember, to Calvary He did go.

And whatever be my lot,
Jesus is the best Friend to be found,
In Heaven, I'll meet my rewards,
But, first the crosses, then the crowns.

The Day the Angels Stood By

It was a day like no other,
The day Christ was crucified,
We know of three crosses on Golgotha's hill,
Two thieves were on either side.

It was a day the Angels stood by,
Ready to obey Christ's command,
They could have freed Him from that Cross,
And removed the nails from His Feet and Hands.

He could have called twelve Legions of Angels,
And they would have set Him free,
Instead He suffered the pain of a Cross,
Hanging on Calvary's tree.

It was day that changed the world,
A day when the Angels stood by,
Yet, Christ gave his life, for you, for me,
And love was the reason why.

Short-timers

A short-timer is a soldier,
Who has just a few more weeks,
Before he's discharged from duty –
And his joy is made complete.

Just as I'm nearing Eternity,
This "old-timer" is a short-timer, too,
Just a few more days to travel,
Just a few more jobs to do …

Until I say "farewell" to this ol' world,
And "hello" to Heaven Above,
For I know I'm going home
To God's wonderful world of love.

The devil's Masterpiece

Hell will be eternal,
There, the cries will never cease,
Without question the damned soul,
Will be the devil's Masterpiece.

In that day, there'll be no turning back,
The soul will be filled with all manner of disease,
The fire will never be quenched,
All because of personal unbelief.

The soul will writhe in pain and agony,
In the torments of the flames,
It will be filled with remorse,
Of unbearable guilt and shame.

Then, everything in Heaven and earth,
Will confess Jesus' Holy Name,
And in Hell there won't be anyone
But one's self to blame.

And the devil will leave his signature
As his mark upon the grave,
And the second death will come
As a Master to the slave.

If the devil claims your soul,
How he'll howl with glee,
As a pawn in the hands of the King of sin,
Sealed will be your eternal destiny.

"For what is a man profited,
If he shall gain the whole world,
    and lose his own soul?"
To tragically face God's wrath unfurled,
And miss Heaven's streets of gold.

Tell Them

Tell the lost of Jesus,
Of how He died to set them free,
Of how He left His Throne in Glory,
And went to Calvary.

Tell them how He is the Friend,
Who will never leave nor forsake,
Of how His Grace is all-sufficient,
And for us will undertake.

Tell them how He'll stand by us,
When even close friends fail,
Of how He is a present help in times of trouble,
When the hosts of hell assail.

Tell them about a Heaven,
Where the saved will go when they die,
Tell them about the mansions,
He's prepared for us on High.

Tell them how Christ triumphed
Over death and the grave,
Tell them how much He loves them,
And of how Jesus today still saves.

Tell them on the highways and byways,
The lost to Jesus win,
Tell them, oh, tell them,
Tell them "for Him."

The Christ of the Cross

Have you embraced the Christ of the Cross?
Have you knelt at Calvary?
Have you known the free pardon of sin,
Of saving grace that can set you free?

Have you given your heart to Jesus?
Once and for all time,
Are your sins washed as white as snow,
Do you know that peace of mind?

Do you know the power that changes a heart,
And Christ's touch that makes you whole?
Has His blood been applied,
To your poor, lost and needy soul?

Have you embraced the Christ of the Cross?
For upon Him rests our Eternity,
He can be your Savior, too,
If you'll but repent and believe!

I'm Going to Go to Heaven

I'm going to go to Heaven,
Without a doubt,
I've trusted Jesus as my Savior,
Which is what life is all about.

Someday, I'll fly right past the moon, sun, and stars,
I will sing and shout,
For I'm going to go to Heaven
Without a doubt.

For all who come to Jesus,
He will in no wise cast out,
Do you know you're going to go to Heaven,
Without a doubt?

Jesus, the Christ

Nail-scarred Hands,
From a heart filled with Love,
So undeserving are we,
To be visited from Above!

Don't Let a Day Pass By

Tell somebody about Jesus,
Don't let a day pass by,
'Till somebody knows that He loves them,
And for them at Calvary He died.

'Till somebody knows that He sees and cares,
And will their sin burdens bear,
That if they repent and believe,
He will hear a sinner's prayer,

'Till somebody knows He'll walk with us,
Until life's journey's end,
That He is our Hope in Heaven Above,
And on earth, our dearest Friend.

So tell somebody about Jesus,
Don't let a day pass by,
'Till the whole world knows God gave His Son,
And we were the reason why.

Oh, the Things That I See

Oh, the things that I know,
Oh, the things that I see,
As Jesus walks through
Life's valleys with me.

My pathway grows brighter,
My life is made complete,
As Jesus walks with me,
The journey is sweet.

Roses are blooming in those valleys,
Even midst the gloom,
For it's in those dark valleys
That faith finds room.

Hope hath arisen in my heart,
There is the breaking of a new dawn,
As God gives me the grace
To carry on.

Such Heavenly things
Are revealed to me,
As Jesus walks through
Life's valleys with me.

The Name of Mother

Charity has hands,
Mercy has feet,
The "call to duty" has a face,
It is "Mother" so sweet.

Compassion has eyes,
Understanding has ears,
Self-sacrifice has a name,
It is "Mother" so dear.

For a good Christian Mother reflects
A bit of Heaven above,
And binds our hearts,
With God's great "love."

Almost Home

I can almost hear the angels singing,
And the bells of Heaven ring,
I'll soon join the Saints in shouting,
The song of victory!

Life's long night has almost ended,
Just a few more days to roam,
There, my loved ones are all gathering,
And I am almost home.

Just a few more trials and troubles,
'Till I sing the song of Jubilee,
For I am almost home,
And it's welcomed sight to me.

This Friend I've Found

Let me tell you about a Friend,
Who'll never let you down,
He will always be there for you,
Leading ever on to higher ground.

He's a Friend who'll walk life's lonesome valley,
Whose love will always bring us through,
A Friend who's made for stormy weather,
And will lead us out to skies of blue.

He'll never leave us nor forsake us,
But, walk with us, Hand in hand,
And when it comes time to cross ol' Jordan,
On the banks of the river, He shall stand.

If you do not yet know Him as your Savior,
There's good news; come gather 'round,
He's will save you if you ask Him,
Let me share this Friend I've found.

His Name is Jesus,
The Savior of Calvary,
When things are darkest,
He shines the brightest, you will see.

For This, There is Jesus

When troubles beset you,
And you are bowed by soul's diseases,
Take heart fellow pilgrim,
For this, there is Jesus.

He has promised to be with us,
Never to forsake and never leave us,
So oft remind yourself,
For this, there is Jesus.

And whatever circumstances may bring,
Just follow where He leadeth,
With new strength in your heart,
You can say, "For this, there is Jesus."

Here I Come on Bended Knee

Lord, here I come on bended knee,
Asking You to forgive,
I come with empty hands,
With only a heart to give.

I know You will not refuse,
A broken and contrite heart,
Give me Thy Peace from Above,
Give me a brand new start.

Here I come on bended knee,
As oft many times before,
As a Father pities His children,
Thy Love is even more.

I bring life's broken pieces,
And place them in Your Hand,
And You'll wipe my tears away,
Time and time again.

Here I come on bended knee,
With my heart grieved and sore.
Pour out Your Heavenly blessings,
On this sinner, so needy and poor.

It is Called Heaven
(but, I Call it "Home")

There, no storm clouds ever gather,
We nevermore shall walk alone,
It is called Heaven,
But, I call it home.

We'll dwell in those beautiful mansions,
And be gathered around God's throne,
As children of the Heavenly Father,
We'll be known as we are known.

We'll sing praises and rejoice,
We'll join that ransomed throng,
It is called Heaven,
But, I call it home.

The light of Christ will forever shine,
Right will triumph over wrong,
The Tree of Life will be blooming,
As that great River of Life flows on.

Sin and darkness will be no more,
Trials will all be gone,
We'll just sit and talk with Jesus,
And know that we belong!

So when this mortal life has ended,
And fallen, all Kingdoms and Thrones,
I will live with Jesus in Heaven,
But, I will call it "home."

The Visible Christ

May all the invisible things we do,
Be enough to suffice,
To point to a lost and dying world
The visible Christ.

Though unnoticed go our deeds,
And obscure remains our name,
We'll do well to remember,
Labor for the Lord is not in vain.

So just keep on keeping on,
In the service of the Lord,
You may turn some lost soul to Jesus,
And rich will be your reward.

You Can't Go Wrong

You can't go wrong,
When you do what's right,
It will lead you out of darkness,
Into God's wondrous light.

It will lead you out of valleys,
To mountaintops of joy,
It will defeat ol' satan,
Who sets about to destroy.

You just can't go wrong,
When you do what's right,
Remember God and you are the majority
In any crowd and every fight.

He will lead you on to victory,
And make your pathway bright,
Because you just can't go wrong,
When you do what's right.

These are the Beautiful People

These are the beautiful people,
Those with selfless giving,
To me, they are "heroes"
Who help make life worth the living.

They are the ones who lend a hand,
To help a brother in need,
Whose charity is evident
Both in word and in deed.

They are quick to come to your aid,
Who know the meaning of friend,
Ready to comfort and console,
Time and time again.

These are the beautiful people,
Just take time to look around,
They're seen in the faces of those we know,
Everywhere love is found.

The Farther I Go, the Nearer I Come

The farther I go,
The nearer I come,
To Heaven's fair home,
At life's setting sun.

My pathway's growing brighter,
With each passing day,
For my loved ones are gathering
Just over the way.

My cross is growing lighter,
And these burdens I bear,
Are nothing at all,
Compared to Heaven up there.

A mansion is awaiting me,
When this life's race is run,
For the farther I go,
The nearer I come.

How Many Mountains Faith Has Moved

At the close of life's race,
It won't be a list of things we've done,
Nor the riches we accumulated,
But, the souls to Jesus we've won.

It won't be the accolades of man,
Nor the feats that we have proved,
But rather "how many mountains"
That our faith has moved.

It won't be fair words or speeches,
But, rather, the power of our prayers,
By which great changes are wrought,
By God who sees and knows and cares.

When we come to life's finish line,
And we meet Jesus face to Face,
We won't stand on our own merits,
But, only by God's mercy and grace.

Calling Home

When I'm low in spirit,
And feel so all alone,
When I need some lifting up
I just call home –

And talk to my Heavenly Father,
About those things that worry me,
And thank Him for the love and grace
Of dark Calvary.

And it cheers my heart and soul,
As if a light's around me shone,
Because I know in Heaven
I'm known as I am known.

And I know my troubles shall pass away,
But, God's love shall endure,
And I know His promises,
Are steadfast and sure.

For He is the Friend,
Who cares and understands,
I can always count on Him,
So I place my burdens in His Hands.

He is my Lord and Savior,
With His blood my sins atoned,
So the times you feel so overwhelmed,
Remember to just "call home."

Jesus Loves Them More

When death claims a loved one,
And our hearts can bear no more,
The saved are safe at home with Jesus,
On Heaven's golden shore.

Though our hearts are breaking,
And nothing silences sorrow's deafening roar,
We can be comforted to know
That Jesus loves them more.

For at Calvary He died to save them,
Just as He did for you and me,
They would not come back if they could,
For they're with Jesus now, you see.

So when you're wounded in spirit,
And your heart is grieved and sore,
Remember, although we love them,
Jesus loves them more.

But for the Cross

But, for the love of Jesus,
But for the Cross,
My soul would be condemned,
And eternally lost.

Nothing good have I done,
No merits can I claim
But, only a simple faith and trust,
Believing upon Jesus' Name.

For at Calvary,
Jesus paid sin's awful cost,
I would be on the road to Hell,
But for the Cross.

Things of this world shall pass away,
And I count them all but loss,
Compared to God's matchless love –
But for the Cross.

All He Ever Did Was Love Us

All He ever did was love us,
All He ever did was give,
He lay down His life at Calvary,
So that in Heaven we could live.

All He ever did was love us,
Yet, they made Him wear a crown of thorns,
He did no sin or wrong,
Yet, He was mocked and scorned.

All He ever did was love us,
And for that He was crucified,
Yet, He prayed "Father forgive,"
Then He stretched out His arms and died.

When the Lights Go Out

Are you going to go to Heaven,
When this life is through?
When the lights of earth go out,
Will Eternity's lights go on for you?

Have you been saved by God's marvelous grace?
Has your heart been made anew?
Is Jesus your personal Saviour?
Do you have a home beyond the blue?

It's nothing good that we have done,
But, because Christ is faithful and true,
When the lights on earth go out,
Will Heaven's lights be shining for you?

A Rags to Riches Story

It is a rags to riches story,
From a beggar to a King,
I have found a Friend in Jesus,
And He is everything.

I was a poor lost sinner,
On the road to a devil's hell,
For the pleasures of this ol' world,
I was willing my soul to sell.

But, one day I met Jesus,
On the road to Calvary,
He forgave my every sin,
And from sin's bondage set me free.

It is rags to riches story,
And, it can be your story, too,
He can truly change you,
And give you a life brand new.

God Shall Wipe Our Weeping Eyes

There, no storm clouds ever gather,
There are no sad good-byes,
There our troubles will be ended,
And God shall wipe our weeping eyes.

There, our trials will be through,
There, we'll sing redemption's song,
Life's long night at last be ended,
And right triumphed over wrong.

There, we'll see our dear loved ones,
Who from this present world are gone,
In that bright, golden tomorrow,
We will finally be at home.

There, no darkness shall ever enter,
And our souls shall never die,
Jesus will be standing there to greet us,
There, to wipe our weeping eyes.

He Never Said

He never said we'd have an easy road,
But, that he would carry our heavy load.

He never said some rain wouldn't fall,
But, that we could find His rainbow through it all.

He never told us there would be no trials,
But, that he'd walk with us the many miles.

He never said they'd be no pain and sorrow –
But, we'd have His Promise of a golden tomorrow –

He never said the sky wouldn't turn gray,
But, rather that it would be worth it all the way.

He never said we'd live without pain,
But, that we could live in hope with a Heaven to gain.

Love Made Our Savior Go

Jesus left His Heavenly Throne,
To come into a world of woe,
Though we may never understand it,
Love made our Savior go.

And sinners still are saved,
By trusting in Calvary's crimson flow,
Which can wash away our sins,
And make them as white as snow.

Oh, what a Savior,
Who nailed our sins to His cross,
He suffered untold pain and agony,
To save a world that was lost.

'Tis the greatest mystery,
But, this one thing I know,
He lay down His life, for our sakes,
And love made my Savior go.

Life is Too Short

Life is too short
Not to be taken seriously,
To live a life for Jesus,
Fully and completely.

To be a friend to others,
To help those in need,
To have the testimony of one,
Who has scattered precious seed.

Yes, life is too short,
Not to be taken seriously,
For our Savior went before us,
And walked the road to Calvary.

We're to turn the lost,
From Hell's fiery abyss,
So no one will …
The joys of Heaven miss.

Eternity Has Just Begun

Written in memory of Paul Maxwell Rhea, - the pride of my life
(March 28, 1978 – October 7, 2000)

with love from his Mom

Paul was a jewel –
Like a pearl of great price –
So great a blessing
While we had him in life.
Loaned to us from Heaven,
And taken through time,
Time spent with him was precious,
Sunshiny days so sublime.
Touched were the lives that knew him,
Souls to Jesus he won –
Now his work on earth has ended,
But, eternity has "just begun."
In our hearts we shall miss him,
Though sorrows to him be no more,
He dwells in peace now with Jesus –
In joy forevermore.

The Relay

For: the Grandkids

When for me life's race is run,
I plan to pass the baton,
With the watchword to those who follow,
"Carry on, Carry on."

To be a good example,
So life's story that they read,
Will have brought Christ the Glory,
Both in word and deed.

To press on to the mark for the prize,
Forgetting those things behind,
To run with patience the race,
Leaving landmarks for others to find.

To run that I may obtain,
To be crowned with the faithful and true,
To be accountable unto future generations,
To you and you and you.

Yes, when life race has ended,
I plan to pass the finish line,
With my torch still burning,
To hand to those next in line.

The Land of Love

Someday, I'm going to Heaven,
To that sweet home Above,
I'll live in perfect peace and rest,
In that beautiful land of love.

I'll see my many loved ones,
Who have gone on before,
Jesus will be there to welcome me,
Standing at Heaven's open door.

All my trials will be over,
And all my troubles will be no more,
God Himself shall wipe away my tears,
When I reach that fair shore.

I shall live forever with Jesus,
In a beautiful mansion Above,
For someday you will find me,
In that beautiful land of love.

The Sweetest Flowers

When life's trials beset you,
And life's ill winds have blown,
You'll find the sweetest flowers
In the valleys are grown.

And the greatest peace of mind,
Is found beneath God's Throne,
For when God walks with you,
You never are alone.

Great mysteries will unfold,
Life's secrets will be made known,
For it's in the valleys,
The sweetest flowers are grown.

Bringing It

Whatever you do in life,
Remember, you only go around once,
You have to really bring it,
So you won't end up a dunce.

Give life your all,
Live it with zest,
Give more than you get,
Give of your best.

Really bring it,
Carpe diem –"seize the day,"
So you'll have no regrets
At the end of life's way.

Then people will say,
"Look, see," he's really bringing it,
With a "reach that exceeds his grasp,"
And enjoying every minute!

God is Not the Author of a Recession

God is not the author of a "recession,"
But, of abundant living,
He's not a God of scarcity and lack,
But of selfless giving.

He is a God of blessings,
Showered from Above,
And wraps our lives,
In His wonderful Love.

And from His "horn of plenty,"
He giveth our daily bread,
The Giver and Sustainer of life,
By His provisions we are fed.

Yet, He is there to aid us,
When our decisions turn out wrong,
A present help in time of trouble,
He gives our hearts a song.

He is not willing that any should perish,
But, that all should repent and believe,
Hell was prepared for the devil and his angels,
But, sinners Christ will receive.

So the next time you want to place the blame,
For us falling upon "hard times,"
Remember Christ came to lift us up,
To peace and joy sublime.

Duty's Call

To: Dad

He answered the call to duty,
Yielding to a Higher Power,
With liberty as his goal,
He realized victory's finest hour.

He fought for a cause
That was bigger than us all,
No sacrifice was too great,
What'ere might befall.

And it was this noble calling,
With a vision that we would be free,
That caused him to lay his life on the line,
And made such a difference for you and for me.

Lift Someone Up

There's no greater exercise for the heart,
Than reaching down and lifting someone up,
It's then God's grace overflows,
And His love doth fill life's cup.

Reach out to someone less fortunate,
Let them know you care,
Bring your petition before God's Throne,
And say for them a prayer.

Jesus said, "If you've done it unto the least,"
You done it as unto Him,
We'll reflect the Father up Above,
Whose Glory doth not dim.

So reach down and lift someone up,
Somebody lost and astray,
Wandering out on the dark hills,
In need of Jesus today.

Say a Prayer

When overwhelmed by troubles,
And burdened by life's cares,
When you need a friend to lean on,
Just say a prayer.

The day will become brighter,
Your cross not so heavy to bear,
When you talk to God about it,
And just say a prayer.

He will open the windows of Heaven,
And pour a blessing to receive,
Nothing is impossible with God,
If we only just believe.

And He will walk with us,
Where no one else would dare,
So when you're tired and weary,
Be sure to say a prayer.

ASAP

ASAP – the acronym, "as soon as possible,"
Could also be, always say a prayer,
Be a first responder,
When faced with worry and care.

Always say a prayer,
When tempted, tested and tried,
Because you cannot fail,
When God stands by your side.

Always say a prayer,
Don't let life get you down,
When doubts and shadows loom,
Find the Friend I've found!

The Man in the Mirror

It matters not what the world may say,
You may receive its endless round of applause,
But, if the man in the mirror knows it's untrue,
You are only a fake and a fraud.

You may fool everybody as you go through,
You may leave "trails of glory" behind,
But, whatever the man in the mirror has to say,
Is surely the tell-tale sign.

You may be very successful,
You may attain fortune and fame,
But, if the man in the mirror doesn't agree,
It's both a tragedy and a shame.

So be true to yourself, what'ere you do,
So that when life's final page is written down,
If you can get the man in the mirror to agree,
You 'll be the greatest guy around!

Hobo

To: Hobo, our sweet little dog, who patiently sat at the computer beside me while I compiled this book!

Hobo is a ragtag dog,
Who came to us as a stray,
From such humble beginnings
He's come a long, long ways.

He's a wire-haired dachshund,
Who has grown quite pleasantly plump
So that when he chases the rabbits,
They now leave him "up a stump."

Into our hearts,
He has made his way,
His picture was chosen for Conway's pin-up pet calendar
Just the other day.

He's got grit and perseverance,
From which we should learn a lesson,
He's now a part of our family,
And we consider him a blessing!

He has plain good ol' savvy,
And he knows just how to get ahead,
I'm afraid the next time you hear about Hobo,
He'll be owning us instead!

Beyond the Bend

It's simple faith and trust
That calms the stormy seas,
It's a faith unwavering –
It's prayer upon one's knees.
These are the things that shake the world,
For God's Power can be seen
When we fully trust –
And when we fully lean.
For He shelters from the storms,
Leads us when we stray,
Brings light to darkest night
And brushes tears away.
For our God sees and knows
Each thing from Above –
And no power can destroy
One covered by His love.
So don't give up when you're in life's throes,
For help He'll always send,
For whatever cup life may hold,
He sees beyond the bend.

Never Say Never

Never say never
When it comes to what God can do,
He can take a sinner's heart,
And give him one anew.

He can mend a broken life,
And turn our gray skies blue,
He will give us grace enough,
And strength to carry us through.

He makes us strong when we are weak,
Gives us faith when we doubt,
And in life's lonesome valleys
He will always see us out.

So step out on God's promises,
He is faithful and true,
And never say never,
When it comes to what God can do!

Will You Finish Well?

It matters not at the close of life's race,
How many people think you're swell,
Or how many medals you may have won,
But, rather if you finish well.

How many souls to Jesus did you turn,
That were bound for a devil's hell,
If you sounded out the watchword,
If you finished well.

You may attain fortune or fame,
But, where life's story will tell,
Is if you kept trusting Jesus all the way,
And if you finished well!

Checkmate?

A young man sat at a game of chess,
He was certain to lose,
For the devil had him in checkmate
Any way, he couldn't move.

The stress and strain were evident,
As sweat lined his face and brow,
For it seemed so certain,
That the man in defeat would bow.

But, another young man looking on,
Studied and pondered the player's plight,
While the devil laughed with glee,
It was truly a tragic, pitiful sight.

But, the young man looking on,
Saw how the chess player couldn't lose,
If he would look unto Jesus of Calvary,
He still had "one more move."

Life is much like a chess game,
But, with Jesus you cannot lose,
If the devil has you in checkmate,
Through Christ you still have "one more move!"

This Could Be the Day When Jesus Comes

I awoke this morning,
With a list of things for self to be done,
But, my plans flew out the window, when I thought,
This could be the day when Jesus comes!

We need to be watching and ready,
And praying God's Kingdom come,
Because any morning, noon or night,
Jesus may come!

Oh, to be found faithful and true,
With souls to Jesus won,
Not to stand before Him empty-handed,
On that day when Jesus comes.

The signs of the times are all about us –
Being fulfilled with very passing day,
"Come quickly, Lord Jesus,"
Should be the prayer that we each should pray.

Let's each set our house in order,
So that when Jesus comes,
He will find faith on the earth,
And God's Will being done.

So let's sound out the watchword,
And teach our daughters and sons,
For ONE DAY, it will be the DAY
… When Jesus comes.

School year 1974-75

Pamela RaNell Hixon was born on June 16, 1951 in Little Rock, Arkansas, to parents Maxine Spryes Hixon and Carl W. Hixon. She has one sister, Tena Hixon, and two brothers, Ronald of Texas, and Rodney of Michigan. She graduated from Conway High School in 1969, and the University of Central Arkansas in 1973, with a BSE in English – her major, with social studies and political science as her minor. Pam had a full scholarship throughout college, and made the Dean's List each semester. She has always loved learning – absolutely. She worked toward her MSE (18 hours) in English at UCA. She received a Fellowship offer for a Master's degree to Princeton where she was invited to teach two classes, but opted to teach at Morrilton High School, English and history, before marrying in 1975. She also taught the school year of 1986-87 at Ford High School in Quinlan, Texas, teaching English and personal business management.

Pam was married for twenty years, being a minister's wife, and was the mother of two sons, Paul Maxwell Rhea, the eldest, and Mark Carlton Rhea. Paul passed away October 7, 2000 due to a car accident. He was saved at age five, and won a friend to Jesus shortly before he was called home to Heaven on October 7, 2000. Mark was also saved at the early age of five and a half. Pam has four grandchildren: Kaitlynn, Gavin and Zack (Mark's children) and Tyler Paul, (Paul's only child) all of Texas. Pam has two nephews, Jacob and Seth Hixon, Ron's children, and one niece, Haley Hixon, Rodney's daughter.

Besides writing poetry, Pam is the keyboard pianist helping with the instrumental portion of the *Faith of Our Father's Radio Broadcast* in which her Dad, Carl W. Hixon has been preaching for fifty years. It can be heard via the Worldwide Web at WWW.KMTL760a.m. and WWW.KWXT1490.com each Sunday morning at 8:30 a.m. and each Sunday afternoon at 2:45 p.m. Family members sing "old-time gospel songs."

Mostly Pam stayed home during the years, caring for her children, learning to give them allergy shots, and cooking up good meals. She feels "at home" in the kitchen, and her latest culinary expertise is making all kinds of good soups. Besides writing, Pam's hobbies include knitting, gardening, reading and singing.

Pam says, "Our purpose in this life is to live for Jesus and win as many souls to Him as we can." The early teachings of her Mother, and the preaching of her Dad all of her life, gave her the foundation for abundant living.

Swan's Song, she says, is her legacy to her grandchildren, all of whom have been saved who have reached the age of accountability.

Pam resides with her sister, Tena, a retired high school guidance counselor. The family made their home in Conway, Arkansas for many years.

To the Reader:

I hope you have enjoyed this collection of poems. To me, there's nothing more "delightful" than composing a poem.

You may write to me at P.O. Box 82, Conway, Arkansas 72033.

May God bless.

With fondest regards,

Pamela Hixon Rhea